LARIONOV

IGOR LARIONOV • JIM TAYLOR • LEONID REIZER

Original Edition Translated
From The Russian By
Margarita Dirks and
Lawrence Fowler

ISBN 1-55056-067-0

Published by
Codner Books
15-1430 Maroons Road
Winnipeg, MB
R3G 0L5

First Printing, 1990

Printed and bound in Canada by
Friesen Printers
a Division of D.W. Friesen & Sons Ltd.
Altona, Manitoba R0G 0B0
Canada

Contents

Foreword iv
A Long Way From Home 1
Voskresensk 15
Archangel 29
Dark Angel 45
KLM 61
Oh, Canada 77
Nightmare! 95
Bombshell 119
Slava 137
Victory 147

FOREWORD

Pat Quinn,
President/general manager, Vancouver Canucks.

It took five years and three weeks of intense, laborious negotiations to get Igor Larionov into a Vancouver Canucks' uniform. The man hours and air miles involved were truly staggering, and until the moment on July 1, 1989 in Moscow when he actually picked up the pen and signed the contract we could never be certain all the time, money and effort hadn't been wasted.

The hunt began in the spring of 1985 when word reached the Canucks that Larionov wanted to come to the National Hockey League. On speculation alone, they selected the gifted Soviet Red Army centre in the 11th round (214th overall) in the NHL Entry Draft. As Arthur Griffiths, son of team owner Frank Griffiths said much later: "We were highly skeptical about Igor coming to Vancouver, but an 11th round pick is always a gamble anyway. In retrospect, it turned out to be a very good gamble."

Now it became a matter of trying to establish personal contact with Igor, to see him in action and find out how serious he was about making the move. In this the club relied on a team director Senator Ray Perrault and Alexei Makarov, a close friend of Perrault and for many years the Minister/Counsellor to the Soviet Ambassador to Canada. Perrault spent months consulting with the Soviet Embassy in an effort to open doors within the Soviet Ice Hockey Federation.

While the Senator worked at the political level, the Griffiths family took another approach. Anatoli Tarasov, considered the father of Soviet ice hockey, and former Red Army goaltending legend Vladislav Tretiak accepted their invitation to attend the Canucks' 1986 training camp on Vancouver Island.

The word they brought with them was not encouraging. Tarasov intimated that the only way Larionov and Vladimir Krutov (drafted 11th by the Canucks in 1986) would ever play in the NHL was if they were first released by the Soviet Army. Tretiak maintained that it was up to the Red Army and national team coach Viktor Tikhonov to let the players go and "only if his future as a coach were assured and not in jeopardy." My own involvement began when I joined the Canucks as general manager early in 1987. Prior to my arrival all contacts were made through the Griffiths family, and even after I arrived they were always heavily involved. Tarasov returned to Vancouver prior to the 1987 training camp to have a hip operation of a type performed here with a very high success rate. Again, he had news: He could assure the Canucks the first Soviet player to the NHL — but NOT one from the Red Army team. So, come June, we drafted Viktor Tuminev, a centre from Moscow Spartak.

I always felt that the key to all negotiations was Viktor Gavrilan, the Deputy Minister of the Soviet Sports Federation. He told me that the Red Army players MIGHT be available after the 1988 Winter Olympics in Canada. All our efforts — written and by phone — to meet Larionov, Krutov and Tuminev, all efforts to make a contractual offer, had been to no avail. But now, with a meeting arranged in Calgary, Gavrilan kept saying "Make us an offer."

So, in Calgary, I made them yet another offer.

"No," said Gavrilan, "we're too busy to consider it now. Wait until after we've won the gold medal." So we waited, and they won it — and suddenly there was no further contact. We were being avoided. But I learned one thing: I learned we had no idea of the complexity of the Soviet system, or just who was at the controls.

In May that same year, the Soviets suddenly invited the Griffiths to fly to Moscow for meetings that would be "significant." I left the Memorial Cup tournament in Chicoutimi, Que., to join them there. Again, frustration. We were presented with a list of 11 Soviet players eligible for release — but Larionov, Krutov and Tuminev weren't on it. Nor was any other Soviet "name" player. That was when we realized who really controlled the players: Viktor Tikhonov.

We arranged to meet him just before one of Red Army's important games. I specifically asked him if he would release Larionov.

"No, not now," he said. "Maybe after the next World Championships."

We realized then that while he was promising veteran Red Army players their release, he was blocking their release. When we left Moscow I was convinced it was never going to happen.

But things were changing, however slightly. Pressure was being applied from all sides: From the players, who were threatening rebellion over promises never delivered; from the NHL clubs who'd drafted them and, like us, had lived through the same broken promises, and from the unwieldy, bureaucratic nightmare of the Soviet Ice Hockey Federation, which was seeing its power slip away.

And slip away it did, in the person of young Alexander Mogilny, who defected and joined the Buffalo Sabres in the spring of 1989.

That same spring we arranged yet another meeting, this time in Seattle. Arthur Griffiths, Senator Pearreault and I sat down with Gavrilan, who echoed Tarasov's earlier assurance that the Canucks would get the first Soviet player. He added that there was also a chance to get Larionov, and asked us to make *another* offer. We did.

Two days later, the Calgary Flames announced the signing of Sergei Priakin from the Soviet Wings.

I flew to the world championships in Stockholm. There I met Larionov, who told me he thought he'd soon have his release. By that time he also had an American talent agent, Mark Malkovich, and an agreement with a European team.

Things were getting more complicated by the day. Cliff Fletcher of the Calgary Flames (who had drafted Sergei Makarov) and Lou Lamoriello of New Jersey Devils (who had the rights to Viacheslav Fetisov) had also been assured that they'd get *their* players out at any moment. Like me, they were ready to jump a plane and fly to Moscow at any moment. (The Devils ended up signing their Soviet players without the blessing of Soviet authorities.)

From day to day we never knew what to expect. We had hockey clubs to run. Did we plan for Larionov, or Krutov, or both, or neither?

Finally, in late June, Fletcher and I were called to Moscow with Malkovich. The meetings lasted two days. Fletcher signed Makarov while I met the Larionov and Krutov families. And on July 1, 1989 — Dominion Day — Igor Larionov became a Vancouver Canuck.

Much has been written about the Russians' first year in the NHL. And it is true that, considering the effort involved, Igor's 17 goals and 27 assists in 74 games were modest totals for all the advance billing he received as a "world class-centre".

But he was in a strange land playing what to him was a strange NHL system of random changes of lines and linemates after a decade of playing on one line and one five-man unit. A change of that magnitude takes time. Hopefully, the glint in his eye as he views his new home is Igor's way of telling us that the best is yet to come.

Chapter 1
A LONG WAY FROM HOME

The house was too big.

Just days ago, "home" had been a two-room apartment in Moscow – two rooms, not one, because I was a famous hockey player, and with fame came some privilege. Now we were in Vancouver, Canada, where I was to begin a new hockey career with the Vancouver Canucks and, with my wife, Elena and our three-year-old daughter, Alyonka, a new life.

And we were moving into this ... this *palace* the Canucks had found for us to rent in North Vancouver: four bedrooms upstairs. A playroom on the main floor, plus a big living room, family room, kitchen, double garage and *three* bathrooms. Only a half-dozen houses in the complex. Behind us, the woods stretched back and up to the freeway.

It was beautiful. Compared to what we'd had, the rooms stretched on forever. But new houses creak in the night. Strange noises come from the woods. Where were the sounds of the city, the comforting, familiar sounds of life in the apartments that had always surrounded us? And how do you fill so many rooms when there are only three of you and one is away as much as I would be?

It was not for Elena. After three months we found an apartment in a new building in a residential area near downtown Vancouver – still huge and luxurious to us, with two bedrooms, living-dining room, laundry room, kitchen and two bathrooms, but on the third floor, with the secure sense of other people nearby, people with whom we might soon be friends. The distances from home are measured in more than miles.

Many circumstances combined to bring about this journey to the other side of the world: Perestroika opened the door that allowed the entire first line of the Soviet National team to come to

1

North America to test itself in the finest league in the world – Vladimir Krutov and myself to Vancouver; Sergei Makarov to Calgary Flames and Viacheslav Fetisov and Alexei Kasatonov to New Jersey Devils –but perestroika has done nothing yet to improve the lot of hockey players at home, to change the festering, dictatorial hockey system that in so many ways forced me to leave. For we who have performed for eight years as Army "officers" for Army pay and those other benefits – a bigger apartment, a dacha (summer cabin), handed out as rewards or withheld as punishments – the money paid us as NHL players would be astounding, the lifestyle as simple or lavish as we chose to make it.

But these alone are not reasons to tear away the roots in your homeland. Really, I left for one reason: Freedom to choose my own path.

A human being has to live in such a way that he feels himself to be a human being – by one's own mind and conscience, no matter where he lives or what he does. To me that has always meant communication with people – not just Soviet people, but people everywhere. I have a need to do this, to relate to people. To isolate, to limit oneself only to hockey, that is not for me. Do it and you will soon regret that in your youth, in the best years of your life, you saw nothing but hockey on your horizon. I could not let this happen. Not to me, and not to my family.

It is a simple thing to say, but perhaps not so simple to understand in North America where such free communication is taken for granted. Let me try to explain.

From the time of our children's team, "Snezhinka" ("Snowflake"), I always preferred the word "rival" to "opponent", which somehow seemed to grate upon the ears. It sounded too much like "enemy", and we were playing a game, not going to war. In the Soviet Union, the long standing term in our newspapers is "friends-rivals." It's a term close to me. I regard the players of the opposing team as colleagues in the hockey profession. In the course of 60 minutes playing time I put out all my strength and ability for the sake of our team to overpower theirs – a team which could be made up of my friends or just acquaintances. Before and after the match, these people are close to me, if only for the simple reason that they earn a living in the same way I do.

Language was a subject quite easy for me, the marks I received were good. Of course, the level of instruction of a language in our normal, non-specialist schools leaves something to be desired. Nevertheless, when on tour as a member of a youth or junior team,

I felt, with pleasure, that I was basically able to make myself understood among the people of other nations. This I considered a happy bonus, a good thing.

Not so. Not to my superiors.

At the Olympics in Sarajevo, I tried to use my free time for making contact. I was rubbing elbows with foreigners, the inhabitants of the Olympic village. However, this natural and harmless pastime for some reason evoked displeasure on the part of Viktor Tikhonov, the coach of the Soviet National team – not the first thing upon which we disagreed, and by no means the last. Finally, when I did not cease my efforts to speak to athletes of other nations, I was taken aside by and strongly reprimanded by Vladimir Yurzinov, a long-time assistant of Tikhonov.

"What could they have to say to you?" he asked. "These are your enemies. Opponents! What could there be in common for them to talk to us about?"

He intimidated me to the point that I was afraid to go to the cafeteria when there were many people there, in order to avoid any of my new acquaintances: Americans, Canadians, Yugoslavians, Swedes, Czechs and Finns. God forbid, that they should see me. I was not the only wilful member of the National team. But I was the only one who could, more or less, express himself in English, the language spoken by so much of the civilized world. Still, new limitations emerged that seemed to be monstrous and absurd to me even then, that today one would not believe.

Like the majority of the other hockey players, I responded enthusiastically to the events unfolding in the Olympic arenas. I rejoiced and grieved for our young men and women. There were many surprises. There were those who received medals and those who were passed by. I wanted to congratulate some and console others, to encourage them. It didn't matter whether I knew them for five years or for five days. But here again our watchful coaches straightened me out.

"It's not worth scattering yourselves about," they told me. "Skiers and skaters have different tasks. They are already celebrating. Their competitions are over. We don't want you to be growing soft. For hockey players, everything is decided on the last day of the Games. Remember this."

It was absurd, but it happened. I hope that it will never be repeated with the generation of hockey players coming up behind us. But even these most stupid and insulting prohibitions or reprimands could not keep us from friendly contact with our foreign hockey colleagues.

Our line upheld good relations with Czech players like Vincent Lukak, Igor Liba, and Darius Rusnak. I was particularly friendly with Dushan Pasek, who was later drafted by the Minnesota North Stars. We'd played against each other on youth teams from 1977. I don't know what he found likable in me, but I can state definitively that Dushan is a hockey gentleman and a strong player, a centre who makes a play happen. He is a kind-hearted, approachable and well-wishing person.

What did Pasek and I talk about? We naturally discussed hockey and the news, our problems and our work. These are our mutual interests. From the contact with hockey players from Czechoslovakia, also a socialist country, we learned that several of our mutual and painful problems apparently were being solved in their country. We envied them in a friendly way.

Another I met frequently was the Swede, Kent Nilsson. Always I came away with a good impression. It goes without saying that Nilsson is a first-rate attacker, but not all stars impress me. Kent was somehow like a member of the family – such a free fellow, open, with a sense of humour and kindness and, it seemed to me, somewhat of a Russian soul. Nor was the fact that he had played as a star for ten years in the NHL ever used by him as a criterion for self-evaluation or a disdainful measurement of others.

Wayne Gretzky needs no introduction. With Vanya, as we call him, personal contact was established almost immediately. Of course, my stock of English words and phrases were very helpful.

What can one learn from such exchanges? As much as you care to absorb. They needn't be long or complex. Bobby Hull, for example, taught me a valuable lesson without ever opening his mouth.

We were in Tampere, Finland, in 1981, at the beginning of my first year with the National side. Our bus rolled up to the arena and was immediately surrounded by fans – young lads mostly, holding out booklets, photographs, scraps of paper and pens, all in search of autographs. I threw my trunk on my shoulder and brushed carelessly through them. But as I headed for the entrance I happened to look up across the crowd, and looked squarely into the eyes of the legendary Bobby Hull.

He was there on a marketing trip. We had never met, and he never spoke. He didn't have to. His eyes sent a clear message: "Hey – a little more friendly, Igor! Don't be so proud! Why offend people? Would it really hurt you to give them a little happiness, to sign an autograph? Would your hand fall off, or what?"

This man who had signed so many thousand himself, whose patience in such matters was a legend of its own ("When Bobby

Hull says his prayers at night," said one writer, "he ends with 'Sincerely, Bobby Hull'") as if by telepathy forced me to stop sharply, turn back, and diligently sign for everyone who wished. Only then, with a sigh of relief, I directed myself to the locker room. Momentarily, I had forgotten the people who are among the most important in our game: the fans. Bobby Hull, without a word, reminded me. What price can you put on communication when it offers a message like that?

I have a shared episode with Gretzky that I'll remember for a long time.

For reasons I will discuss later, I had become politically undesirable and ineligible for foreign travel with the Soviet Red Army team (CSRA) and thus with the National side, since Tikhonov controlled both. In December, 1986, I was in Canada for the first time since 1984, to play in the Calgary Cup, a competition run by the Olympic Committee in that city as a build-up to the 1988 Winter Olympics. The journalists wasted no time seeking an answer to the Big Question: Why had I not played for such a long time outside the USSR?

I dodged and kept silent, and because the tournament had no real significance I got away with it. But two months later when we arrived in Quebec City for the "Rendez-vous 87" tournament, the situation had changed. The organizers called a press conference. Six members from each team were invited, Canadian and Soviet. We were seated in the presidium. Our whole line was there, and there was no escape.

The Big Question came again: Why had Larionov been so long away from the international arena?

I said what I thought. Until now, I told them, the situation had not been made clear. The stories, the excuses offered by others, were not true. There had been no "chronic illness." There had been no incident with a girl at the 1984 Canada Cup competition, as had been charged in a Quebec newspaper just before our arrival for Rendez-vous – although had there been, it would hardly have been a crime.

The article claimed that in 1984 after our 3-2 loss to Team Canada in the Canada Cup final, I met with Wayne Gretzky, Larry Robinson, Mike Bossy and Michel Goulet in a bar. Yes, and Alexander Kozhevnikov of our squad was also with me. And allegedly we were there with women. The journalist claimed that Gretzky had organized it, and that Gretzky himself had given the journalist the information. Because of this, allegedly, Larionov was not eligible for foreign travel.

The Canadian players were interviewed first. Naturally, Wayne was one of them. After they finished he rushed over to me.

"Believe me, Igor," he said, "I didn't say what was printed in the paper. I'll tell them it didn't happen. But what IS your position now?".

I told him what I thought to be true. After all, I was again allowed to travel abroad. I was again a member of the National team. It was 1987, and 1984 and the Canada Cup seemed far away.

And what had been my "crime" back then? I had simply voiced my opinion, told the truth. In interviews they had arranged here and there, I said that I like the organizational work in the NHL, and I liked the people in the U.S. and Canada, who were most hospitable. Then someone asked:

"What do you think, Mr. Larionov, will you ever play in the NHL?"

"Yes," I answered. "In the near future, I think, contacts between Soviet and Canadian hockey players will be closer and our players will play on NHL teams."

After the 3-2 loss in the final, we spent three days in Toronto. There the coaches arranged a team meeting. Obviously, the interpreter had made them aware of this article in which my "anti-Soviet statements" appeared. In the course of half an hour they raked me over the coals. Tikhonov branded me an evil enemy. He seemed to blame me for our loss to the Canadians. I was at fault! How could I have behaved so? It was a most genuine badgering.

Although I am a calm fellow, all the same I worried about it inwardly. It is very painful when in front of everyone they find you guilty of all the mortal sins. It was absolutely undeserved. Because what sin had I committed? In Canada as at home, on and off the ice, I simply wanted to be what I was: a human being, with his own thoughts and opinions. I was asked those questions, and I answered them. But this seemed to be prohibited.

Still, I thought, all that was a long time ago. It could not be hung over me forever.

"Do not worry, Wayne," I assured him. "Now everything is okay."

I was wrong. Everything wasn't okay. For me, the biggest battles lay ahead.

Why did I want to leave the Soviet Union? Why, in October, 1988, in the popular magazine OGONYOK, did I write the savage, open letter to Viktor Vasilevich Tikhonov blasting the inhumanity of his hockey system – and, indeed, the system above that allowed it to flourish – and flatly stating that this was my last season under it, when I knew it could end my hockey career in the Soviet Union and didn't know if I'd ever be able to get out to play anywhere else?

Why, in that same article, did I expose to the world the issue of the injections in the training prior to the 1982 World Championships in Helsinki, and the doping control cheating at the games themselves? There were many facets to that article, but this was the one that exploded like a bomb:

"Well, by what cost is victory achieved? The superior (Tikhonov) as a rule is not interested in that! Is the 'physical' preparation in order?, is what you discuss before the players. And 'your emotions interest me little.' The point! The 'physical' some times is also not in order. Then enter bio-stimulators.

"You remember, such a noise was raised when I refused to take an injection before the 1982 World Championship in Helsinki that they even reported it to Goskomsport (the ruling body for Soviet sport). *For the honour of the line, neither I, nor Krutov, nor Fetisov, not Makarov, nor Kasatonov, wished to enter a new level of play by such methods; and we did not* (take the injections) ..."

This was a hit below the belt. However, I did not break the rules, I went against those people prepared to break them in their preoccupation with our preparation.

The injection process always began three or four weeks before the championship, at the CSRA training camp, with the shots given over the period of five days to a week. We didn't know what was in them, but we had our suspicions. I flatly refused to take them, and after this refusal before the Helsinki tournament I was never asked again. But others went along – and were still doing so at the Moscow championships in 1986 – afraid of losing their positions. And Tikhonov left no doubt about that.

After the first training session at which we had refused the injections in 1982, Tikhonov had a behind-closed-doors meeting with the doctor of the National team,who had been summoned urgently to the CSRA.

I remember well the threats from the lips of the hockey monarch:

"Whoever does not take this injection, I will report them to the sports committee. We will decide the question, right up to the dismissal from the National team!"

Those were his words which, as they say, you cannot take out of the song. We were not told exactly what was in the injection, because a doctor administered it. Without doubt, they had some sort of agreement about this incident.

All of my own doubts ended in Helsinki when I saw how the doping control tests were circumvented.

Everything had been thought of ahead of time to eliminate drug use through foolproof methods of detection, which would lead to default of matches and medals, and ultimate suspension. Or so the tournament officials thought.

Those selected for random testing – I among them – arrived at the doping control centre and were given a jar. A laboratory assistant accompanied each player to the washroom where the urine sample was obtained, making sure that the player did not substitute anything (like a pure sample) brought in with him.

That was the theory. For the Soviet players, the procedure was somewhat different at the end. When I went into the washroom with the laboratory assistant, he reached behind the toilet and came out with a jar already containing a urine sample, obviously pure. Wasn't that efficient? We didn't have to dodge the test – it had already been done *for* us!

We waited a moment, then went out into the testing centre, where I handed the officials the new sample bottle, and left. For me it didn't matter, because I hadn't taken any injections anyway. But I knew now what must have been in those injections – or else why worry about rigging the test? And where, you ask, were the medical representatives of the international medical federation? They were presiding over the tables in the testing room. The laboratory assistants who accompanied us to the washroom were ours, Soviets.

With the article in OGONYOK, my lot was cast. To Tikhonov, all suspicions and feelings were now confirmed: I was the enemy. Yet I knew this would be so. Why then did I risk it?

Perhaps Mikhail Gorbechev's rise to power in 1985 had something to do with it. As with the majority of professional hockey players, I do not consider myself to be an expert in politics. But I admit at once: I believe this man. I liked his face, his manner of behaviour. I was impressed by his ability to speak freely, without a text, from both the high platform or at ground level, rubbing elbows with the people. But the main attraction was the plans he put forward to lead the country out of a difficult position. One could sense that an active, intelligent man had come to power.

I had a somewhat enthusiastic perception of the new leader of the country. I read, listened, talked, discussed and argued, and I was happy that a time had come when people could calmly and easily speak out. Because it could apply to hockey players, too.

Until perestroika I felt hopeless. It was a blind alley. The way ahead could not be seen, it was not clear where it would lead me. For impudence they could cut down a whole career. They could make you ineligible for foreign travel, or banish you to a military posting. It was simply done, and you were left without recourse. I knew that in the new conditions in the country someone could support me. It wouldn't be so simple to take the law into their own hands with a hockey player as before. I could stand up for myself This was a massive awakening of human dignity.

The other factors pressing in on me and influencing my decision had little to do with hockey. Again, it was a question of life and the manner in which it should be lived.

I made the decision myself to part with the Central Red Army (CSRA). No one asked, and no one prevented me. I love and respect my parents and I value close friends. With Lena, thank God, I can discuss anything. But I'm more comfortable making my own decisions. Long ago I was given counsel on which to base a life: Make all important decisions in the morning. I would think about the problem, calmly fall asleep, and in the morning with a clear head the problem would be settled. As the proverb says, "The morning is wiser than the evening."

I had many acquaintances. I make contact with people very easily. But in times of decision, special friends are required who, after honest discussion, will offer good and intelligent advice. These, like so many things in my country, were in short supply. In the year that I became so suddenly and inexplicably undesirable; when after a hundred tours and tournaments I was a second-class hockey player no longer deemed fit to travel internationally, gossip and rumours swirled around, and I learned a bitter lesson.

Most people immediately turned away or became distant. Some kept in touch, apparently just in case, while awaiting the outcome. I had friends, good friends who did not turn away: Two or three in Voskresensk, not hockey players, but hard-working people in ordinary jobs. We rarely saw each other, much more rarely than in our childhood, and the times will be even rarer now. But they will always be there for me, as I will be here for them.

And I had my teammates – but in truth, not all of them. True friends – but not as many as I'd thought.

And there was the waiting, and shortages, and the lining up for things that often weren't there when you reached the head of the line.

When we arrived in Vancouver we were immediately befriended by the team captain, Stan Smyl, and his wife, Jennifer. Naturally, the press was watching our every move, and much was made of a shopping trip to a local supermarket. It had been decided to have steaks that night. Jennifer threw enough for the meal into her shopping cart, then turned away in seach of something else. When she turned back, Elena was piling all the steaks from the freezer.

People laughed at the story. But in Russia we have learned that what is in the store today will not be there tomorrow, so you buy as much as you can when you can. The idea that she could come back to the same store the next day, and any day, and find the shelves stocked again was something Elena could not yet imagine.

Let me take you with me on a shopping trip I made in Moscow in the summer of 1989.

I had finally quit the army, saying goodbye to the coach who could all but cause in me an allergic reaction just by coming into my sight. I was occupied with questions regarding the signing of the NHL contract with the Vancouver Canucks. I was living at home, with my family. Every day I saw my wife and daughter. I could help them, take care of them and be with them from morning to night, and from night until morning. something I could do only rarely in the structured hockey life.

The early morning began with "cross," a series of special exercises, and then swimming the Moscow River, after which I went to the milk store. Alyonka does not eat very much. She seems to be following in her mother's footsteps, a figure skater who strictly watches her weight. But there is something Lena likes – a milk drink, "ryazhenka," which she can drink all day. She also likes "kefir." (fermented milk). And so I hurried to stock up on these simple products, also buying butter, eggs, and cottage cheese. A routine exercise, you say. But imagine this:

Let us say that on a particular day I returned home with a real "find": ten small two hundred gram bottles of "ryazhenka". I would understand that tomorrow there would be no more of it for sale, but there would be kefir, and the day after tomorrow there would be neither one nor the other.

When time allowed, I would drive to another store – but there they might have milk and cottage cheese, but no other elementary things that Alyonka required. And no matter where I shopped, or for what, it would take a long time. Because everywhere there are lineups. If there is no lineup, then it is not worth going to the counter, because it means there is nothing left.

I would know that my daughter would be fine even without the "ryazhenka," as long as she can play with her daddy and talk with him, but it still does not sit well with me to return home with an empty bag. My mood is already ruined for the day. I am tired of these stores where you do not know what awaits you; where shopping for essential things is a matter of blind luck. I am tired of the eternal lineups, the everyday companion of the Soviet people. I am tired of getting quality products only with the help of people you know or in the foreign currency store "Beryezka."

And I can see no changes for the better.

I perceive this whole primitive daily existence very acutely as a degradation, especially after trips abroad. Why do the Finns, the Swedes, Czechs and Canadians not have even a hint of these difficulties? Why are we, the Russians, afflicted with them?

Once Alyonka became ill and we called a private doctor. (If you can afford it, the quality for health care is totally different than that in the government institutions. Some doctors in the government hospitals also do work after hours, for payment under the table. It is often said that the quality of health care is much better "after hours.")

This doctor advised me to get some disposable syringes. In other words, to get something which is readily available in civilized countries. You would go to the drug store, to any one of dozens of drug stores, and pick them up without thinking. In Russia it is easier to shoot a bear.

I began to hunt for syringes. I could not buy them anywhere. Friends of friends had promised to get some, but no one knew when and how many, and I really prefer to rely on myself. In the end we were lucky. The team went to West Germany, where I was able to go to the pharmacy and get as many as I needed.

There is a disturbing addition to this story. Soon after my arrival in Vancouver I arranged to have 10,000 such syringes shipped to Voskresensk. I sought no publicity, but a story appeared in PRAVDA in Moscow saying it was being done. The syringes were shipped – but they never reached Voskresensk. Where did they go? In my country, who can say?

Why am I telling you about these shopping odysseys? Our lives are made up of little things. Decided or undecided, they usually create our mood. With the Soviet people, alas, it is the everyday

11

little things which shamelessly take away their time, and strength, and mostly their nerves. Little things that added to the pile of factors that led us on this journey around the world.

I will tell you one more story – or, rather, let Elena tell it.

My wife is a former world champion figure skater in the ice dancing pairs, a title she shared with Alexei Solovyov in both 1980 and 1981. As such she has travelled much of the world herself. She knew the strains I was under in my battle with the hockey system, and she knew first-hand what life was like outside our borders. Listen, then, to a small part of her side of that story:

We were moving into a new apartment – a two-room apartment, double what we'd had. We did not have many things, but Vladimir Krutov was there to help.

"I've found you a deal," he said. "They'll move all the furniture without a problem. Get everything ready, and don't be long."

Igor, as was agreed, stopped at the transportation agency on Byovaya Street to complete the arrangement. An hour passed, then two. I was beginning to worry. After three hours, he called and said he was now third in line. I went to him and we stood there for another two hours. Five hours in line for a mover. And they say a hockey player has pull!

This has never been a shock for me, the three of us living in a tiny apartment, since many sportsmen live like this, and some even have two children. It was our visitors who were surprised – especially foreign correspondents who came to visit or interview us. The American TV personalities, it seems, could not believe their eyes. Neither could the plumber who came to the apartment after the housewarming.

"Do you really live here?" he asked.

"Of course," I said. "Who else?"

He lifted his hands in dismay.

"You know," he said, "My apartment is much better."

Igor is liked by reporters, Still, when these Americans came, I felt embarrassed. They were from some TV show, I cannot remember from which company, doing a documentary about Soviet hockey and interviewing Makarov, Larionov and Krutov in their homes. In this they probably saw additional significance.

The whole group came over in the evening. About five people: cameramen, sound operators, and others. At that time we were living off Polikarpov Street, next to the central hippodrome, in a one room apartment – a little flat, would be more exact. When the Americans began to place the equipment, they probably decided that this room was the hallway, and that the living room, bedroom and chil-

dren's room were further back. As if that were not enough, that there was only one room, we had also divided it with a curtain, behind which were unopened boxes containing the new imported dining room set from Yugoslavia, which would stay packed until our move simply because there was no room for it.

They got their interview, but left shaking their heads: How could a world hockey star live in these conditions?

I myself viewed them calmly. Especially after Alyonka was born, I would have liked to live in a three-or four-room mansion. But I had to remind myself that I lived in Moscow and not on some distant island or somewhere in heavenly Switzerland. I have seen how some Moscovites live. I knew that there still are more than a few "kommunalki" (communal flats) where two or even three families dwell. I also knew very well that many sportsmen live as we did. The family of Stas Leonovich, many times a prize winner at a World and European championships in pairs skating, also huddled in one of these, and they had two daughters, one four years old, and the other two. They were feeding them with promises for a long time. He was already a trainer with the CSRA, and lived like this

I also understood something else. After Igor was invited to the CSRA, they gave him a two-room apartment with his parents. One must take that into consideration. In Moscow you remembered everything, especially if you have received some sort of benefits already. And my husband had received this "wedding" apartment after we were married.

What I did not understand was the way apartments were distributed. If there is such a thing in a country that a person cannot take or buy the apartment which he liked and could afford, then they should also distribute the dwelling space fairly. How? Seemingly, according to merit. And here much seemed strange to me.

Why did the Kasatonovs, for a long time already, live in the beautiful three-room apartment in a good stone house in the good part of the city while the twice Olympic champion Larionov does not even dare dream about that? Lesha Kasatonov received this prize when he was 25 years old, moving into, by the way, Tikhonov's former dwellings, and Larionov at 28 had to knock on many a door just to get a two room apartment.

Or, for example, Konstantinov received a comfortable living space when, forgive me, his child was not even born yet, and the Larionovs, already three of them, lived in one little room? Well, forgive me, but who is Konstantinov and who is Larionov? Konstantinov has played at a World Championship twice, many said only because he was playing with Tikhonov's CSRA and obeyed him irrevoca-

bly. Was it fair, this "sorting out" to see who got what apartment? This is probably naive on my part, to wonder at all this. Naive because I really know how everything is done. Everything depends on one person. On Tikhonov. On his will, his mood, his personal relationship with this or that hockey player. But what about merits, pure sports merits? If he wants to, he will take something up into his attention, if he does not, he will do nothing. He has ho superior over him, no one to stand in his way. He's the boss! I ask: Is this fair?

And now, at last, we were here. Kurtov also, although he would soon go back to get his family. In a matter of weeks, he and I would be trying to show fans of the NHL that Soviet hockey players could play with the best on a regular basis.

I knew it would not be easy – for us, or for Fetisov and Kasatonov in New Jersey, or Makarov in Calgary. The Larionov Line was no more. When next we met it would be as rivals. Not as opponents. After eight years together, we could never be that. Rivals, playing our game on a new stage, looking back sometimes along the path that brought us.

Chapter 2
VOSKRESENSK

My journey to the NHL began in the hockey capital of the world.

Not Moscow, or Montreal, or any of the other Canadian cities where the game can be said to have its roots. A dilapidated little one-street town – since grown to two – called Voskresensk, a chemical complex 88 kilometres from Moscow, pop. 80,000, where a team emerged in the 1950s and immediately was a force to reckon with. Voskresensk. My home.

The team was called Khimik, and it was not so much from the town as part of it. On game days it seemed the small stands could seat the whole of the town – or, in any case, the men. Countrymen my father's age thought it was great fun to knock off the state's favorites: the Central Soviet Red Army (CSRA), Dynamo, Wings of the Soviet – all from Moscow; Torpedo, from the city of Gorky, and the Sport Red Army (SRA) from Leningrad when they were highly regarded. And Khimik tried very hard to please the citizens.

One of the big teams would come for a game, and the next day in the central press information would appear about the latest "disrespectful" step of Khimik, the latest surprise. In the early years no one took it seriously. "Coincidence," they said. After the latest steam-rolling in Voskresensk, the leaders of the distinguished clubs needled each other: "Who are you kidding? How did you manage to lose to one street?"

I know these things to be true, because Nikolai Semenovich Epshtein told me. "Semenych", as we called him, who built this team with his own hands and mind, did not have the habits of exaggeration or distortion. And today, a quarter-century later, there is evidence all around that it is still a fact.

Not that Khimik won championships. You have to be a little tough guy to contest for a medal in the course of a long season. Usually Khimik did not hold out. But giving the leaders a battle, especially in our own rink, was the sweetest thing. We from Voskresensk proved that we were no fools. This feeling was passed

15

on from generation to generation. I felt it most flying home from the 1988 Winter Olympics in Calgary.

I had been totally focused on the games themselves. It was as though I saved my emotions in order to let them out on the ice. I left satisfied with myself. Satisfied with our squad, our team. We won there, as they say, without question. And then, on the flight home, I napped for a while. When I awoke and looked around, it was as though I was somehow back in Voskresensk.

To my left Valeri Kamensky was dreaming, to my right Sasha Chernykh was thinking about something. In the seat two rows in front me of was Andrushka Lomakin, face buried in a newspaper. I know them inside out. From Voskresensk, all of them. The Olympic hockey champions, and among us no fewer than four fellows from my city, or better yet, my town.

And you know, the fellows from Voskresensk were not spares. I state this without any false modesty. In North American hockey a "line" is the three forwards, and the lines may change while the same defensive two remain on the ice. In Soviet hockey a line is two defencemen and three forwards. A team is 22 players – two goalkeepers and four such lines of five, and the lines always change as a unit. Kamensky played a keen attacker, Lomakin a tactical manoeuvering forward and Chernykh a competent freewheeling play-maker on the second line. I played as usual on the first line. Adding it up, I was surprised myself: a quarter of all the attacking strength was represented by us, natives of Voskresensk. Pride for my native city overwhelmed me, and I felt as I had when I was a little boy, after our team Khimik had taught the CSRA hockey team to run as fast as they could.

Is it possible that there is something similar on a national team from Canada, Czechoslovakia, Sweden, or Finland – a town that size contributing so many ranking hockey masters to a national team, a team that claimed gold medals in almost any tournament? I doubt it. I doubt it very much. On the hockey map of the world, my Voskresensk would have to be identified not as a small spot, but as a large, beautiful circle: the hockey capital of the world!

This story brings a smile to some people's faces. For me, it makes me proud. Pride for one's own place of birth, for one's family, and for the small unspoiled town that wiped the nose of anyone. Say what you may, but I will always have an overabundance of patriotism for Voskresensk. Whether in the Soviet Union or abroad, I am prepared to argue with anyone that Voskresensk is something unusual in hockey. It's a phenomenon!

16

But why is it so?

Voskresensk to Kiev. Voskresensk to Riga. These are not names of railway lines. These are the comparisons which beg to be compared. Riga, the capital of Latvia, is a large city, a cultural centre rich in tradition. People there have long been accustomed to hockey, and this has moved them into the middle division of the game in Russia. Hockey prospects look incomparably better there. But, who shines from Riga, who is invited to the National teams? Balderis. Helmut Balderis alone. But he is a forward, a God-sent forward! But who was trained there, what is the characteristic trait of Latvian hockey? Personally, I do not know. Or Kiev, a beautiful city, a great city, a sports-minded city. The team Sokol has existed there for about seventeen years. It has won the USSR Championship. Yet not one memorable hockey player has come out of this club.

But from Voskresensk – from Khimik? Alexander Ragulin! One of the best defenceman in the history of Soviet hockey. Yury Lyapkin and Alexander Pahskov of the 1976 Olympic champions. All discovered on the Khimik club. And the list could go on. Should one of my countrymen take it into his head to build a museum for the hockey greats of my city, visitors would see something special!

In the Soviet Union, perhaps only the Urals, only Chelyabinsk is a competitor for us. This is where Makarov, Bykov, Starikov and Mylnikov are from, and all were also on that 1988 Olympic team. But, if you compare Chelyabinsk and Voskresensk in size, they are comparable to an elephant and pugdog.

But what about my native town? What is at the bottom of the Voskresensk phenomenon?

It is difficult for me to explain. It is a matter of traditions, and they were made before I was in this world. And even today I play as before; I do not observe and analyze while calmly sitting somewhere with a note pad or a video camera.

Everything began here with the appearance of Epshtein. Nikolai Semenovich Epshtein. I consider him a specialist on the scale of the legendary Anatoli Tarasov or, Chernyshev. I know him well. Although he was never my coach, he was a friend of my father and was always attentive to me. He gave me wise advice, and I took note of it. At that time he no longer worked with Khimik, but all the same he supported them, for the team was his life's work, and he cared for its continuation. He treated me like one of his own.

He had his own approach to the game, a zest, an instinct for players, an understanding of them. He valued players, those who knew how to play hockey. To play – but, not to run at neck-breaking speed all over the ice, or only to get underfoot at every step. He loved hockey players with finesse, technique and mobility. If he did not see an up-and-coming candidate in the city, he would search the region. So by bringing together the raw talent of the youngsters, he would train them by his own standard.

But, still, how he found them is inconceivable. He turned his attention to Yury Lyapkin during the summer at some match or other at a championship in the Moscow area – for soccer. They say that Yury, when he appeared at the Khimik club, could not skate at all, and the others wanted to hold him up.

Semenych did not copy his technique from anyone. He preferred playing on the defence. Let's say the CSRA team came to Voskresensk. It would include about half the national team, including at least two lines of attackers. And what attackers: the Almetov line, or the Polupanov or the Petrov. To try to match them on attack would make no sense. They would tear his club to pieces. So Semenych first of all built a precise and elastic defence, designed to confine the zone of movement for the CSRA stars and catch them with counter-attacks. Thank God we had someone to carry it out with intelligence.

The typical Soviet coach gives the impression that no one has taught him, no one inspired him to a general thought. He seems to feel that the players themselves do not understand anything, that they must be told what to do or they will mess things up, that there is no keeping them in check, that all they think about is violating an order and making mischief. He feels that he has to be able to pull on them as if they were on strings. You think for them, you care only for those who prove their worth in a game. And, most important, the coach's authority is beyond discussion.

Semenych had his own principles. He had a clear head, the old men tell me, and did not like to scream, and did not like to take revenge on anyone. Semenych helped as much as was within his power in solving everyday problems: getting an apartment, or a car. In dealing with adults who, as hockey players, were literally undefendable and without rights, he dealt humanely.

Players instinctively were drawn to him. They believed his promises about everyday living and they listened to him as to a specialist. They were prepared to turn themselves inside out on the ice, in order to please "our Semenych."

Truthfully, Epshtein did not very much possess the appearance of a coach. He was small in stature, neat, with an intelligent outward appearance. In his youth he himself played soccer, apparently, quite well. He had met on the field with Bobrov himself and other postwar stars.

And he must have been a diplomat. To convert an out-of-the-way, God-foresaken little town into a hockey centre he first had to convince directors of the chemical plant that was our town's main industry – men who had not even heard of the pastime – to support this foreign game. Epshtein knew how to do this.

Gradually our little town began literally to live by hockey. Interests evolved suddenly and constantly around the game – not only among male fans, but among youngsters, retired people, and even among women.

In Voskresensk they tell a story.

A woman walks into a store and discusses the latest news with the sales clerk:

"I heard that Ninka had triplets!"

"That's so."

"They say that Semenych found out about it. He was pleased, and said 'We will prepare an attacking trio out of them.'"

In such a town I was born and raised

Actually, our family lived on the outskirts of the Lopatinsk suburb, about five kilometres from the city. Only later we settled in Voskresensk.

My mother is from the Gorky region, from the country. She is from a peasant background. She toiled away from dawn to dusk, taking care of the family. In general, she forgot about herself. What did she see in life? Endless hard work and troubles. What could she allow herself on a wretched eighty rubles a month? Nothing. It all vanished without a trace. My mother is sick. She has high blood pressure. I do not see her often, but I love her very much and she is in my heart, in my consciousness; she is a real Russian woman.

And, I am attached to my father. He is a hard worker, a slogger. An honest man. Easy by nature. He was a lathe operator. Now, he has plunged all of his time into the construction of our "ranch", tearing down the old house on a dacha lot not far from Voskresensk and building a new one. (It was not unusual for players on the national team to be given such dachas. Kasatonov, a suporter of Tikhonov, was one who received such a reward. I hoped for years without success. Finally, I gave up and bought it myself.)

I do not remember when exactly I began to skate. My parents are at a loss to recall. They had other troubles enough. But I know

I could not have passed by hockey even blindfolded. Everywhere, on the streets, on every sheet of ice, boys were chasing a puck until they were dizzy. Anywhere you listened, the only conversations were about last night's or tomorrow's match. These hockey waves swept up everyone.

Last year I purposefully used the side streets in driving through the whole town. In one street, even though it was the middle of October, street urchins were chasing the puck on the pavement. I drove through many streets, but saw only the one hockey game. In my childhood it was the other way around, you could not find an empty school yard or street. We didn't wait for winter. When they sent us to a collective farm to harvest potatoes, we would grab a few nets and make goals out of them and use a tennis ball for a puck, sprinkling the pavement with sand in order to reduce friction.

There are two roads to hockey – and to all other sports – in the Soviet Union: For the masses, the street; for those considered exceptionally gifted, the special sports schools.

Let us first deal with the schools. Each sports club – CSRA, Dynamo, Khimik etc. – has its own such school. At age six, boys are brought to school "tryouts" by their parents and watched by coaches and members of the adult teams. Those considered to show promise – a boy who skates well or appears exceptionally well co-ordinated for the sport – are invited to attend the special school. Here they attend regular classes in all subjects, and these are in no way neglected. But hockey is also a subject well taught. They begin the day with hockey training from 8:30 to 10:30 a.m., attend regular classes from 11 a.m. to 4 p.m., then finish with another hockey training session.

But this is for those considered to be potentially the future best. The mass hockey program is, literally, a competition of the streets.

A man on one street – not a professional coach, just a man interested in the game, might want to coach a team. He would go to the boys on his street and sign them up. These boys are from nine to 15 years, and divided into age groups.

This man and other interested people, parents of the boys, perhaps, flood the playgrounds, help the boys clear away the snow and set up and coach the games against other teams from other streets. It is much the same as the North American minor hockey system. The boys go to regular school for their regular five 45-minute classes, go home, get their homework finished, and go to hockey practice. From these games come playoffs – district, city and eventually between champions of the various republics in the country.

But it all begins with a man, not a professional, who is interested enough to want to coach.

Elena and I have had both views. I went to regular school and played in the street leagues, but there was also a hockey school I was able to attend for training. As a promising figure skater, and later a world class competitor, Elena went to one of the special schools. It is hard to make a choice except perhaps in this: Elena hears from me good memories of my school days and the things we did – a walk in the fresh air, a game of something else, an after-school activity. She has none of these. For her, school memories are all of training...

The schools serve their purpose, but to me school yard games were the great things. I am judging not merely by my own experiences, but by those of my partners, who joined street hockey games in Moscow, Chelyabinsk and Leningrad. It is wonderful when a young boy, hardly conscious yet, gets used to the game in the open spaces, outside in the fresh air, without instructions and shouts from the coach. You just go outside and chase the puck until your legs give out. You do not want to look bad among kids your own age. You really want to stand out, and afterward also in the company of those who are a head taller than you, you do not want to have mud on your face. Instinctively, you look for some sort of method, some elements you can install in your game, some moves to help you excel.

One of the reasons I advanced through the ranks to the top Khimik team with success was the confidence learned in the streets. When I stepped on to the articifical ice I did not feel like a newcomer. I knew about competition. I'd learned it in the school yards.

Krutov has also played his fill of street hockey near his house, almost in the centre of Moscow. Makarov began to sharpen his own formal dodging technique on his Chelyabinsk street. His parents did not even place him in kindergarten. "Why?" they asked. "He is in view all day under the window, playing hockey." Fetisov came to the famous CSRA school for children and youths with a solid street hockey career behind him. And Kasatonov at first was trained in the swimming section, the only one of us who tested himself in another sport. He has also played on the street for a long time, but often, it so happened, without skates – our damned deficit in almost everything. (We can get skates and sticks, but parents make their own face masks for their boys, and pads and other equipment come neither in quantity nor quality).

We lived in a one-bedroom apartment – my mother and father

and my brother, Zhenya – in a nine-storey building. From those who lived in my building alone came two who play as pros: Sasha Chernikh lived a floor lower, but Vitya Donskov was a neighbor in the next apartment. Without realizing, I had introduced them to hockey. A chain reaction occurred. I was a little older, already on Khimik's top team, and they followed me, one after another.

Andrei Lomakin also came. There was a four-year difference between our ages. I was already playing captain, and I felt somewhat like a leader, but I still liked to hang around with the boys from the street. I noticed a young boy skating by himself. He'd skate every day in a mohair hat and sweater which his mother had knit for him. Andrushka was six years old then, and growing up without a father. I felt like helping. So, I asked Dmitrich Odinokov, who was my coach from age seven to 17, if Andrei could study under him.

I had fallen into good hands with Odinokov. He was attentive and did not scream. From childhood on I could not bear it when they screamed at me, especially when voices were raised when there was no need. It is possible Dmitrich is not on the list of professionals of children's hockey, but what was good was that he allowed us to play as much as our souls desired and did not torture us with remarks. Even in my mid-teen years with him it was as if my street hockey days continued, only on a more serious basis. Dmitrich agreed to let Andrei join the team and Andrei began to grow, and grow, and play, and play. Then, when I had left for the CSRA team, somehow he dropped from sight. But we met again on the National team. Where else but in Voskresensk is such a thing possible?

As they say, there is a time for everything. I was 17 and felt my own backyard getting too small for me. I needed a greater hockey challenge – which meant that I had to break into the top Khimik team. Easy enough to say, but there were hundreds every year who dreamed of the same thing, and in the entire town only one team in the top league. But I made it – partly, perhaps, beause I had an advantage. I had come under the influence of Nikolai Semenovich Epshtein.

Semenych has since passed away. I never did get to ask my childhood teacher why he had taken a shine to me. Whatever the reason, I am grateful. His influence on me was great. I listened to his concrete instructions or advice, but I particularly liked his unorthodoxy. I tried to live by my own mind, but Semenych nudged me, as if invisibly, to search for my own way in hockey, and life in general. I missed him terribly.

My wife was at one time looking through our family album.

There was mother still young, and father also, and Zhenya. She came across a photograph of when I was 13, in a hockey uniform, sitting on a bench, resting between changes. This is me in Cherepovets, in the final of the All-Union tournament, the Golden Puck. We, the natives of Voskresensk, had placed first! The forwards on our line – Volodia Solovev, Sasha Gribanov and myself – had received the prize for the most points. The prize was from the newspaper PIONEER PRAVDA. (As grown-ups, Krutov, Makarov, and I received similar prizes for six successive years.)

Then we actually became the best in the country for our age group. But then we finished school and went our separate ways. Solovev and Gribanov did not make it on Khimik, and joined somewhere in the second league.

Why did it turn out this way? You can not say at once. I was smaller than the rest in stature, the thinnest, but on the ice I always had the primary roles. It became more complex for me when I was about 14 or 15. Everyone else began to grow like weeds and played with the advantage of gained strength. But I almost did not change at all. The coach must have thought to himself that I stopped growing. Solovev and Gribanov grew stronger, and it was pleasant to look at them. They stood out more than I did: they rammed on defence, pressed into battle, ran around as if just out from the sauna. Sasha is, by the way, the nephew of a well-known hockey player, Yury Chigurin, who was a very talented attacker. His technique was such that you could not take your eyes off him.

Two years passed. I had grown a little, but that is not the main thing. The main thing was the ability to think, to see a range, to possess technique. At 16 or 17 you have to have your own style. If you do not have it, then you must somehow strive for one and polish it later. You must develop willpower, ingoring all other temptations for the sake of hockey. It was as if at that moment Solovev and Gribanov stopped in their hockey development.

In the senior classes many guys were trying to pump up muscles, to make their figure more athletic, to look masculine. This is quite natural. Given the nature of the game, it would also have been natural for me to provide myself with a few dumbbells and weights. But, for some reason this idea never appealed to me. I knew my own playing strong points, and tried to use them to the fullest. They did not revolve around raw strength. Had I pumped up, I would have increased my weight and then skated around with extra kilograms. I didn't need that.

Who made an impression on me? Who had shown me something useful for me? Vladimir Shadrin from Moscow's Spartak, also a centre, also a genuine playmaker. Our Voskresensk, Volodia Lavrentev, a sly technical player. And of course, Valery Kharlamov.

I learned easily. For some reason I like the English language, I never thought how it would come in handy in the world of sports. I quickly grasped the new material of other subjects also, but it turned out that I would not go any deeper in my studies. Hockey took up an increasing amount of my time and strength. Sometimes an uncanny fatigue weighed me down. Early in the morning, after my parents left for work, I would cling to the window and watch how many of my classmates were going to school. If a lot were going, thus making my absence less noticeable, I played hookey – and hockey. My school teacher, seeing how torn I was between school and hockey, showed great understanding. But when my mother discovered my slyness, she began to ring home to check up. To avoid the strumming of the telephone I would lie down and disappear somewhere in dreams. For ages I could not sleep enough.

In general, though, the transition into adult hockey happened rather smoothly. I held my own in classes. It helped quite a bit. I did not lose my way. I knew what I needed. In contrast there was my brother, older than me by four years. He played not badly at all. We were similar in stature and also in style of play. But Zhena inwardly, as I now understand it, was not very strict on himself. This appeared in everything; every trifling thing was important. Well, in our business there are no trifles. Zhenya did not immediately make it into Khimik, and he did not want to wait. He joined a periphery team, a team totally lacking in discipline. Things went from bad to worse. Nothing decent has come out of my brother. It's too bad. Otherwise, somewhere they would have written: "The Larionov brothers are from Voskresensk."

Finally! The childhood dream was fulfilled. They gave me a complete canary yellow uniform. I was on the Khimik team in the top league. I played for four years (1977-78 to 1980-81), four wonderful years in front of my fellow countrymen in the city I loved, the city where hockey was king.

And then, regrettably, it was time to go. Why is it then, you might ask, that I agreed at 20 years of age to desert my native home and go there, where much was foreign to me, not to my liking, where reality, alas, turned out to be even worse than I waited for with anxiety? Because there was no other way to move up, to test myself in a larger hockey orbit.

It has long been the way of Soviet hockey: the strong clubs grow stronger at the expense of the modestly supplied. They downright rob them. It is done in the interests of the bigger club, or for the promotion of the player himself from a remote place. And for those players who dream of playing for the national team, all paths to "hockey Rome" lead, unfortunately, to Moscow. Specifically, to the Leningrad Prospect No. 28, the site of the Central sports club of the Army – since time immemorial the core of the national selects team and the only door to it.

In no other civilized hockey country is there a joint coaching hierarchy in which one man coaches, at the same time, both the leading club and the national team. Only in the Soviet Union.

But it was an inescapable fact. And so I set off on the road to the geographical capital, Moscow, with a hockey duffel bag and other belongings, to try to open that door. Two months following the joining of the CSRA team, I was already playing in enormous, filled-to-the-brim Canadian arenas, playing on the National teams of the USSR, on the squad which was judged to become the pride of our hockey. Would Tikhonov really have taken me into this very squad directly from Khimik? Never in a million years!

And yet, after having joined the CSRA team, and immediately after that the national team; having already tasted huge victories in Canada, at the World Championships in Finland and West Germany and at the Olympics in Sarajevo, in my heart I had not left my native city, my home club. I am not saying this for the sake of sounding pretty. I played on a line that in those years destroyed everyone, one after the other. The Larionov Line, it was called, after the centre. (And, in North America, the KLM line, because our three initials matched those of the Dutch air line, and who could deny that we flew?) It would appear that all this glitter, all this overflowing happiness from the game and the pride from the victories, all the cities and countries that I have been to, all this fame --and, why hide it, the noticeably improved material prosperity and a whole new lifestyle – had to overshadow or at least push the memories of a modest Voskresensk sports palace for some three thousand spectators into the furthest corners of the mind, along with my street, my home, my friends and my acquaintances. Ah, no. It all lives inside me, it warms me.

There is a saying, "To go away in order to return." In my soul I have remained a native of Voskresensk. For me, any trip was a joy, a gulp of fresh water. On hockey business, as a member of the CSRA returning to play against my native Khimik, I did not experience any sort of mixed feelings. I am a professional. I still have these feelings from the time when I played for the youth teams. I do my job, like some worker of that chemical plant who works conscientiously. Therefore, it is a lot worse for me when I don't score against Voskresensk. Usually I was completely indifferent as to who scored for our squad. Against Voskresensk, I tried to stand out. In one such game I scored in the second-last minute of play and it ended 1-1. I had no regrets. The people of my town were not offended. In principle I could not make a blunder in my native city. Four thousand viewers in the stands, and I knew almost all of them. They didn't simply look familiar; I knew them by name! The thing is that, with a city like ours, everything revolves around hockey. If I did not give my best, then I would be failing them.

A problem with drinking exists in the Soviet Union, and my native city has not turned the corner on this problem, this evil. Once a middle-aged fan who was a little tipsy came up to me, and addressed me as if we had known each other for a long time. In fact, it seemed that I had seen this face before.

"Igorek, our dear Igorek," he cried. "Well done, you didn't let us down. You upheld our colors, Voskresensk! Be so kind, give me three rubles and I'll drink to your success. May you continue to beat them!"

What do you think, that I recited him a lecture about the harm of alcohol? No, no. This first time I was taken by surprise, and immediately I dug into my pocket and gave a three-or five-ruble note to the well-wisher. Later on, such scenes ceased to surprise me. Such was the coloring of Voskresensk. Here my childhood friends live and prosper. In all of the eight million Moscovites, you could not find a person who could measure up to them. Friends, I have in mind real friends, there cannot be many. And these Voskresensk guys are my wealth, my support in life. In life, which from year to year does not become any simpler.

My city drew me there like a magnet.

Now it is so far away, life is so different in North America. And still I miss it: sitting with my friends and talking about life at a bar in the centre of the city, the only decent place...the real Russian bathhouse, and spending half a day there with my old dear acquaintances of all ages listening with curiosity to my affairs, about my travels in the whole wide world. And to me, their modest concerns are near to me as before...driving to Lake Egorvsk in the summer for great swimming, or fishing, or solitude. This was all mine. My roots.

Sometimes the drive to Voskresensk would be for sport – but not for hockey. My city would want me for a soccer match in the championship of the region, not for the extra attraction my popularity would bring, but for the help I could bring the team. Among hockey players, I was highly regarded in soccer. (But not in the summer of 1989. Pat Quinn had phoned me in Moscow, warning me not to take any unnecessary risks, to avoid the possibility of injury. Already, the North American move was bringing changes.)

Once, about six years ago, I slipped away for a couple of days in Voskresensk and found my old coach, Dmitrich Odinokov, in the nearby small town of Lukhovitsy, not so much coaching the local team as organizing it. And who was the team playing that day? The adult team of Khimik – coached by none other than Semenych. Yes, yes, Epshtein was spending his time with semi-professionals as a hobby. Still, no matter how you look at it, it was an official game, the championship in the area of the Moscow region, with 500 fans gathered.

I could not resist.

"Can I play for the Lukhovitsy team?" I asked. "It will help me loosen up a bit. They won't do as your rivals anyway."

Semenych smiled.

"Okay, go!" he said. "But only if we agree that you play defence."

Well, either I got excited or my modest partners jumped higher than their heads. We administered a complete rout to the Epshtein team. And the rumor spread all over Voskresensk: "Have you heard? The Lukhovitsy guys beat us cleanly. And even having Epshtein himself did not help!"

In the winter of my final season in Moscow I drove once again to Voskresensk, negotiating a plan under which I might come home to stay.

I did not hide my intention to try for a contract with a team in the NHL. But I knew the road to Canada would not be smooth. Fetisov, Makarov and I were merely the first at breaking a path which would not be smooth for a long time to come, and not one of the Soviet functionaries who held our fate would say how, or if, the matter would be concluded. Therefore I offered my services to Khimik IF the negotiations with the NHL broke down. Was it a bargain? It was a bargain! We agreed without a problem, like gentlemen.

Fate, however, smiled on me. On the 1st of July 1989, I signed a contract with the Vancouver Canucks. The agreement with Khimik thus collapsed. And my fellow countrymen? They understood perfectly, even coach Vladimir Vasilev, who had expected my help. Again, as nine years earlier, they ardently wished me success. Back then, the route was 88 kilometres. Now it was over 10,000 kilometres to Vancouver.

It made no difference. I was their countryman. And wherever I was, they knew that Voskresensk would always be with me.

Along with my luggage and my family and my dreams, I brought one final memory of Voskresensk.

It was the fourth and last meeting between Khimik and the CSRA in my final season of Soviet hockey. And Khimik had beaten us not once, but all three times. Beaten us cleanly. Not for a long time had anyone done such a thing, beating the base club of the national team. Each time it was called a sensation. As in the 1950s, Voskresensk could now tease Tikhonov:

"What is this? Beaten by two streets?"

Surely in this last match, with the approaching end of the season, the Army would take revenge, win at least once against this insolent Voskresensk team. In this match the press called a war, Tikhonov would have it no other way.

It did not quite happen. It ended in a 3-3 draw. In four matches against the base team of the national squad, little Khimik had gone 3-0-1.

Immediately after the match, having quickly taken a shower, a rumpled hockey player hurriedly left the dressing room with the team emblem "CSRA" and went into the dressing room marked "Khimik." He congratulated the Voskresensk team on the draw, which was as good as a win. He was the first to congratulate them.

Now, who do you think that was?

Chapter 3
ARCHANGEL

I never wanted to join the CSRA team. Never.

Even then I was someone who understood a few things, and could make reasoned guesses about others. And what I heard and guessed about the army team and its new coach, Tikhonov, was enough to give me grave misgivings about playing my game under a military regime. Our Volodia Lavrentev was already assigned to the National team. According to him, the picture under this new man was not coming together very nicely.

I believed Volodia, and as a player I was infuriated at this gathering of the best players to one club team – not as the National team, but as a club team (CSRA) that would serve as its base and thus have a clear advantage in regular competition – and controlled by the man who also coached and controlled the Nationals. More than anything I wanted to develop into a master player and, together with my fellow Voskresenskovites, beat the CSRA. To me, it would be the fair and proper answer to an obvious injustice.

But still, as a school yard player I was used to thinking for myself, living by my own mind. And, after all, this Tikhonov who had come to the CSRA about the same time I graduated to major hockey, was head of the National team. Did I dream of making that team? Of course I did. I had seen this man only on television. I had no idea of his coaching philosophies, the demands he would put upon his players. Perhaps if I met him...

I got my chance in a way I never expected.

Late in the 1980-81 season, the mighty CSRA team came to Voskresensk to play Khimik. I was not terrified by the prospect. Why should I have been? The name of our boys' Snezhinka team thundered through the Soviet Union and I was a member of its top line. I had played on the national youth team that won the world junior tournament during the 1980 New Year's holiday in Finland

and was voted by the coaches of all the teams there as the tournament's outstanding player.

In a way, that was part of my problem. That title meant something to me. The feeling of leadership burned in my blood. Unfortunately, with arrival of adulthood, many of our players left serious hockey behind, and a town as small as Khimik could not continually produce replacements. I was not used to losing, and during those first years in Khimik, when I was still undecided on my hockey future, any defeat wounded my vanity. And I especially suffered when we lost to the CSRA.

About 90 minutes before the game, I was standing outside the rink with my Khimik teammates when the CSRA bus rolled up. As usual, it stopped not far from the door of the arena so the players could get off and walk around. I nodded to Lesha Kasatonov and Slava Fetisov, but stayed where I was as the CSRA team moved toward the door. I noticed out of the corner of my eye that for some reason Tikhonov had moved off in another direction and out of sight.

"Igor! Come here."

It was was Boris Shagas, the head scout for CSRA, beckoning me. We moved off together, turned a corner – and there was Tikhonov himself, waiting.

He wasted no time.

"We want to invite you to our team," he said. "We have certain definite hopes tied up with you. In the CSRA you will be able to fully discover your potential. Do you understand the situation, eh?"

I nodded silently.

"So – here with Khimik you will play this one match, then the next five games you can rest. But this is still not enough in order to develop. Nikolai Drozdetsky has come to us from Leningrad, and look at what he has become. And, if you leave for another team, it is all the same, we will draft you into the army. If you will be on the CSRA team, you will be on the National team! In general, Igor, think it over. Weigh it all carefully. We are talking, you know, about your future."

I said: "Good, I will think about it."

This "dark alley" did not improve my mood, it worsened it. Yes, I dreamed of playing on the National team. But I dreamed of going directly to the National team from Khimik. I seemed to be between two magnets. Each one pulled in its own direction: quickly agree to such a tempting proposition and go to Moscow; or, stay in my native city, on my own team, and live so that my soul would be calm? Just thinking about it made me dizzy.

Why hide it? Tikhonov's words had stirred something in me. The dream had become more than a half reality. Against this pushed a distinct feeling that I would be rather afraid of the CSRA. This dependant life horrified me, this army membership, and the corresponding inner regulations. But the other prospect – of turning down the invitation and attempting to rise in the hockey structure elsewhere while doing my two years' compulsory military service – somehow did not tempt me at all.

There was another worry, until then pushed to the back of my mind.

I had spent two years on the national youth team with Vova Krutov, and already respected him as both a player and a person. After youth appearances we would return to our home teams – he to CSRA amd I to Khimik. We rarely saw each other, but I was happy at his quick and confident adjustment in major hockey. Still, I confess to a feeling dangerously close to envy.

After that world junior tournament, he barely made a stopover in Moscow before he left for Lake Placid to join the Olympic Games team and earn a spot on the National squad. But not I. Larionov, the tournament's outstanding player, was not taken anywhere.

I will not say that I was disappointed in the end, that I was ruined, had lost sleep, appetite and peace of mind. No. All of this was somehow quickly put in the background – but never quite out of my mind.

Did I dream of the National team? Of course. Any somewhat decent hockey player, if he is still sufficiently young, wants to distinguish himself from guys his own age, wants to see himself in the uniform of the National team of the USSR. I wanted this very much. Very much. But time passed, and nothing definitive came to light concerning me. True, during the summer of 1980 I was invited to the training camp in Staiki, which is near Minsk. However, I viewed the situation realistically, and considered the possibility of me making it into the ranks of the National team, as before, as problematic.

Now it seemed the opportunity was mine. All I had to do was reach out and take it. All I had to do was ignore my misgivings, leave my home, and put my fate in the hands of this Tikhonov.

The night I met Tikhonov we tied them 5-5 and led the whole game, but the refereeing was clearly prejudiced and kept us from the win. I was walking tall that night. The tie was as good as a win. Our line played against the Makarov-Zhuktov-Krutov line and outscored them 4-2. I did not score, true, but, if I am not mistaken, I made five assists.

I made no particular effort to distinguish myself in front of the national coach. My mind was totally in the game, in the battle. I completely forgot about the conversation that had preceded it.

Several days passed. The tempting offer did not leave my head. I understood that in the CSRA some of the veteran aces were finishing playing, and the chances were high there to attain a distinguished position. I pondered who would be my linemates. To the left, it was clear: "Krut".

But it would still be the CSRA, and I had another option: Spartak, coached by Boris Pavlovich Kulagin, started to work on me to join that team.

Boris Pavlovich Kulagin, knowing how to approach a person, was very persevering and amiable. He talked with my parents, led them to the director of the first Moscow auto factory, a company that had taken the Spartak team under its own little wing. In Russia there was a five-year waiting list to buy a car. Did my parents wish to do so? Somehow, they could find themselves on the top of that list. Kulagin even led me to a little produce store and piled salmon and other tasty delicacies into my Zhugli.

I gradually came to the conclusion that, no matter which way I went, I would be abandoning Voskresensk. Khimik survived worse times. Yury Ivanovich Marozov was the manager of the team, to whom I am indebted to this day. He was a good coach, but his very trustfulness and tactfulness worked against him. Had he been less gullible, Yury Ivanovich might have achieved more recognition as a coach because he might have had more dedicated professional players at his disposal. But given the existing circumstances, I myself doubted whether I could add up to anything in the game.

The problem of a choice remained acute. The CSRA, which had almost guaranteed me a place on the National team? Or Spartak, from where the way to the National team would be a long and winding road? To Tikhonov who, politely speaking, caused me to prick up my ears with an instinctive distrust? Or to Kulagin, who did not cause any sort of negative emotions, but who, rumor had it, was no longer held in favor by the hockey authorities?

I couldn't reach a decision. Semenych, who had transformed a remote town into a hockey capital with his own hands before I was even born, stepped in. His tone left no doubt:

"Go to the CSRA," he urged. "Throw out these doubts! There they will give you stars on your epaulettes, and secure your future. And you will get on the National team."

I trusted Semenych as my father, as myself. In such a fashion I was rendered a volunteer in the military service.

Oh, how I did not want this army hockey forced existence, this ordering about, when it is impossible for you to make a peep. But even today I think that I had no other way to try to explode on to the hockey scene. Truly, all the hockey roads did lead to Moscow's Rome, to the CSRA. If a fellow dreamed to dress in the sports shirt of the National team, then scarcely could he avoid possession by the irreproachable authority of Tikhonov. In this I could see nothing good. But there was no other road. So, with much misgiving, I became a private in the army, and a member of the CSRA.

On the CSRA team or the national team, I did not feel like the worst player. From the first day of my appearance on these teams, I was consistently placed on the first line. In some areas of the game I looked better than the rest; in others, possibly, I was inferior. But in one thing I surpassed them all: the difficulty I had putting up with the country training camps, at the live-in hell called Archangel.

North American hockey players complain often that the season is too long, that there are too many exhibition games, that with training camp included the hockey year can stretch from mid-September to the end of May for those fortunate enough to be in the Stanley Cup final. And these complaints are not without merit, considering the amount of travel involved in this league spread all over the continent. But in North America, pre-season training camp lasts only two weeks. In Europe it is much the same. Camps are moved from town to town, the training held in local rinks where the people can come and watch. There is hard work, but there are breaks. At night, before curfew, your time is your own to wander those towns as you please, providing of course that you do nothing to abuse the privilege.

But let me tell you about our training camp and season. Let me tell you, first, about Archangel...

It is not a place without beauty. It is set on banks of the Moscow River, about 35 minutes by car from the ice rink, and from the outside looks not unlike an expensive, three-storey motel surrounded by forest and park land. Actually there are three separate areas within the fenced-in complex: the hotel and training centre, a museum and a retreat or spa for high-ranking officers in the Soviet Army. There is a separate gate for each area. They are always locked.

This is the training camp of the CSRA hockey and soccer teams. Beautiful, is it not?

We live there, and train there, for better than nine months of the year. Preliminary training begins June 25. The actual training camp opens July 15 of one year and ends on May 5 of the next. For all of that time Archangel is our home – except when the selects are moved on to the National team, which lives and trains at the Novogorsk centre for the Olympic teams mid-March to mid-April and again in the first two weeks of December.

Come inside our nine-month home. Here on the first floor we have the cafeteria, the sauna and medical rooms, a recreation room with a TV set and an old pool table, and the foyer. The second floor is the residence for the soccer team, the third for the hockey. There are 18 rooms per floor, sleeping two players per room. Each room is big enough for the two beds, a night table, a lamp, and not much else.

Toilets? Of course: two per floor. Telephones? A private one for the coaches and trainers, and two more – one per floor, at the end of the hall, for the 70 soccer and hockey players.

Home? Oh, yes, we could go home – every Sunday until Aug. 1, and after that one evening every 10 days or so, depending upon the feelings of Tikhonov. But be back in time for the morning exercises at 7:30! And, again depending on the senior coach, sometimes our families or girlfriends were allowed to come to the camp for a day visit, during which we could walk in the park or sip tea.

And how did we spend our time in this wonderful atmosphere?

Up at 7.15 a.m. Exercises and controlled running begins in 15 minutes and runs for 25-30 minutes, followed by more exercises for another 45. Breakfast at 9.

The team splits into two groups, alternating times daily. Group 1 begins with weights at 10, ice time at 11. Group two gets the extra hour after breakfast and does weights at 11 and ice time at 12:30.

Lunch for Group 1 at 1 p.m., for Group 2 an hour later.

Rest. Half-hour drive to rink for practice 5-7 p.m. Drive back for supper and massage.

Line up for telephone. Watch TV, play cards, read.

Curfew 11 p.m. Goodnight, Igor. Tomorrow you can do it all again.

This routine was not without variety. In July we had more weights and running and exercise work and less ice time. Preparing for matches and tournaments, less exercise and running and more ice time. Variety, as they say, is the spice of life.

Salary? Ah, yes, we were paid: 350 rubles per month, plus a bonus per victory of approximately 100 rubles. One American dollar is worth six rubles, so the base salary would be just below $60 per month, with another $16.66 for every win. But, do not forget – we had all that wonderful room and board at Archangel – free!

I do not want to leave the impression that only CSRA operated in this manner. All sports clubs had their training centres, their regimentation. But in this Voskresensk was a good example: The hotel, training centre and home were all close together, and downtown. You had breakfast, lunch and dinner at the hotel and trained at the centre, but you could go home at night, as long as you were back in the hotel for the 11 p.m. curfew. Not a desirable way to live, you will agree, but at least you had the nightly home associations. You could be with your family.

It was the militaristic approach of the Army clubs – and, at CSRA, the attitude of the senior coach – that made life unbearable. As to why such an existance is tolerated even in the city clubs, it is simple. We have known no other way. The country cares for and feeds its athletes, and for this the athletes are expected to perform. The teams are picked by the coach, who is also the person to decide which players get the rewards, the presents. This was the same in every sport, not just hockey. As a world-class figure skater, Elena was enrolled in a similar program at age 11.

There was a reason, we were assured, for the stricter regimen at CSRA. It was to prepare us for the games, to keep us from distractions, to keep our thoughts centered around hockey, the task at hand. We were supposed to breathe the forest air and refresh ourselves. I was prepared to accept all that when we were talking about, say, the forthcoming world championship or the Super Series in Canada. But the rest of the time such training is an anachronism, an indication of distrust of the player and a clear and unsightly proof of his lack of rights.

I endured it for eight years, fighting the system whenever and however I could. It was as though I were in chains.

When my baby, Alyonka, fell ill at home I could not even help my wife. I sat like a fool at the camp.

An interesting theatre premiere in Moscow? I don't have to worry about tickets. I was sitting in Archangel.

A journalist asks to have a meeting with me. I have to keep postponing it. Archangel.

Want to call home? Don't be late returning from practice. There was only one working telephone on our floor, and in the evenings the lineup in the hallway was huge. Unless you were one of the lucky ones able to get there early, you could be left waiting for an hour or more, shuffling your feet impatiently, waiting for a brief contact with the outside world.

This artificial isolation enraged me more and more with every year. We continually stewed in our own juices, in boring surroundings where the evening leisure time was spent in front of the television, or playing cards, or shooting pool on a table threatening to fall apart at any moment. How could there be any aesthetic development, any cultivation of the personality. We had only each other, and the walls of Archangel.

Eventually, such treatment alienates you from the real world. We grew used to having everything prepared for us. Judging by the previous generations, this complicated the later years after sports, a problem which has not been socially solved in the Soviet Union anyway. I am a grown man, a husband and a father. In the Soviet Union I actually never – never – helped around the house, even if there was enough strength and desire. This was unnatural. Irritation was building up inside. But the hockey enslavement did not allow us to break out of this closed circle of training camp, league matches, tours and training camp.

A naive question: what is needed for strong hockey players to get pleasure from the game? I can answer for myself, and at some level for the entire Fetisov-Kasatonov, Makarov-Larionov-Krutov unit, who are all now in North America: In all those years, we never found it comfortable.

Nowhere was this discomfort more acute than in the relationship between the directors of the team and the players. In us they saw subordinates, obliged to win without end. Subordinates completely without rights.

We were always playing on the brink of exhaustion, especially emotional exhaustion. Rarely, very rarely, were we actually in high spirits, in a good frame of mind. And that is when we received pleasure from the game, and when we played our best. But never did those directors understand that, had they shown us some humanistic attitudes, some elementary respect and attention, trust and concern, we would have given the spectators a significantly more enjoyable time – and had one ourselves.

I am a dispatcher – a centre, they say in North America. My job is to feed the wingers, to establish a combination play involving the whole of the line. Playing for the youth hockey team of Khimik I rarely scored; I didn't have the strength yet, nor the mastery, and Voskresensk hockey was not experiencing the best of times. But, it was all compensated for with daring and the happiness in trying! If, in particular, the goal of CSRA – the goal of Vladislav Tretiak! – was successfully unsealed.

Now there I was on the opposite side, playing with the CSRA team, playing on top of the world! In the Army club everything was more solid, even the prospects of almost everyone of getting onto the National team. Every player was of special talent and strength – a star! Moreover, I was lucky enough to get onto the first line right away. And I began to score, and score more often that ever before. And the beautiful combinations ran high.

For the first and second year the realization of that high scoring was enough. Then the euphoria began to dull a little, and with my native city never totally out of my mind, I came to a startling realization:

I got more happiness from the game when I was playing for Khimik.

On Khimik I considered every goal scored as a weighty contribution to the success of a far-from-brilliant team. The reactions of my fellow townsmen, from little to great, I felt in every fibre of my being. On the CSRA everything was different. Every achievement, goal or outstanding play, was thought of not as an accomplishment but as something expected. Was it not what I was there for? Even the reaction of millions of fans of the hockey flagman was more out of habit and less poignant.

I do not deny that in the years of my zenith I experienced fantastic happiness. Happiness in creating a play in the company of Fetisov, Makarov, Krutov and, at some level, even with Kasatonov. Happiness in improvising and at the same time achieving enormous goals. But the keenness of emotion, the feedback from the spectators that was part of the very fabric of the game at home was missing here. And without it, why then dress in the beautiful uniform with the enormous star of the almost incomparable champion – why then play on the best squad in the world?

And the irony is this: For all this organization, this determined concentration of the best on one club to form the basis of the National team, I'm not entirely sure our line wouldn't have played just as strongly for the National team had Makarov and I remained where we grew up. Arkadii Ivanovich Chernyshev, who together with Anatoli Tarasov had won world recognition for the Soviet hockey school, wrote that, "if they are great masters, they will find mutual understanding, after a couple of training sessions they will learn to play together." So might it have been with us.

The National teams of Sweden and Czechoslovakia are made

up of players from various clubs. There are even players from teams that are not particularly brilliant. Is Von Gustaffson a strong player? Yes, but he plays in the second league in Sweden. True, but he helps the National teams immensely. Here, as in economics, we show our poor organization: There are talented people playing in the provincial towns, but no one ever thinks of them.

In war, soldiers are taught to accept orders without question, and perhaps that is how it must be. But though we were technically in the army, our purpose there was to play hockey, and hockey is a game, not a war. Thus, for someone of a questioning nature, someone who looked for the logic of things, there were times – many times – when the reasoning behind aspects of life in Archangel seemed ludicrous. I simply could not understand those who followed blindly.

Consider two aspects: training, and food. I had my own training beliefs and my own diet, and I was a successful player from the moment I arrived. Does it not seem logical to let me continue in the manner that is so obviously working for me?

But no. Not at Archangel.

Victor Zhluktov did not shine as a player, but thanks to his faultless obedience to Tikhonov, he got on to the National team with no problem. I had barely joined the CSRA when he began to bait me:

"Hey, what is this? A centre forward who cannot lift weights?"

He was correct. I did not lift weights, and Zhluktov did. I did not accept the opinion of those who placed a powerful torso and impressive biceps as the main yardstick, and for that reason many doubted my prospects as a National player. But I played for eight seasons on the world's best line while the tall, heavy-set Zhluktov continued to work with his weights and peacefully spent his years as a secondary player on the National side. So what did Archangel teach him?

But if my lack of weight training bothered the directors of Archangel, my manner of eating must have infuriated them. Because the fact of it was and is that I just don't eat very much.

After a match, players would go out for a meal and have meat. Why? It is only harmful. The body spends a great deal of energy processing meat, energy that should really be saved. So, I myself take fruits and vegetables, and not whole plates full. But, the next morning I can allow myself a hearty breakfast.

I am not saying everyone should do this, only that it is the way

38

I believe best for me. But the National team coaches could never see it that way.

"What's up?" they'd demand, staring at my lightly-loaded plate. "Eat like everyone else! Drop your Epshtein tricks."

Ah, Epshtein. It is true, my Voskresensk coach did have a great influence on me. But even as a youngster I tried to look at everything that concerned my training and my hockey development. If nourishment restored strength and energy, which a hockey player used in large amounts, then surely one had to approach breakfast, lunch and dinner with thought, and not mechanically empty plates as the majority of players do. And as a player who depended upon speed and agility and didn't place importance on size and strength, I did not want to increase my weight any more than I wanted to pump away with the weights and add to my muscles.

I have listened to the advice of people who knew a thing or two about the questions of nourishment. And some things I have figured out myself.

There was much chuckling and teasing when I first came to the CSRA. "What a strange fellow!" they said. "He eats like a bird! What kind of a trick is that?" After the training session they all hurried to the soda water machine, quickly drank about two or three glasses and hurried to a hearty dinner. And I unhurriedly chewed on a small carrot, greens, an apple and a small orange. And that would be all for the next hour or two.

Once it became apparent that my eating habits weren't preventing me from playing at the top level, they stopped with their little jokes. But no one wanted to adopt anything from my system, which I stick to even today.

Seven hours prior to the game I eat a salad and maybe a small piece of meat, and then stop eating altogether. I might drink something, but not much. And that's all. After the game – water and juice, three glasses but not gulped down, and some fruit.

Krutov did ask me once to help him lose a little weight. Vova is powerful, a go-getter, excellent tactician, and utterly fearless. But with his build he has a problem: He is too big, even for his type of play. Sometimes he surpasses 200 pounds, compared to my 165 pounds, and we are both 5'9".

"Okay," I said. "Let's fast for a day. I will keep you company."

We did not pick a good day. We were flying to West Germany, and the time zone change added another two hours. In the morning, we had nothing but water. When the attractive stewardess distributed breakfast, Vova manfully refused. We arrive in Cologne, where the team ate again before training.

"Igor," he begged, "can I eat a little something?"

"Nothing!" I insisted.

"Well, can I have some consomme soup? A little bit?"

I could not bear it.

"If you want to refresh yourself, have some consomme," I snapped. "And you might as well have everything else too."

He drank some consomme, but did not touch the second course. We trained. He survived on water for supper. I was proud of him.

The next morning at breakfast, he filled his plate to the brim. What works for some obviously doesn't for others.

My other linemates? Makarov began to follow a diet without my influence. Fetisov did not eat much, although in my view he wasn't too discerning about what was good and what went with what. But, in general he kept himself lean and in good form. Kasatonov did not know at all how to restrain himself at the table.

I believe I can offer proof other than hockey statistics that my system of diet works for me.

In October, 1988, I fractured my right ankle during a league game. For reasons I will discuss later, my hockey future depended a great deal upon how quickly I could recover. I went about it in my own way, assisted by a nutritionist and a specialist in Eastern medicine. Neither was any sort of medical wonder, but both were thoughtful, attentive, independent thinkers.

I starved for three weeks. I only drank water, and when it was completely unbearable, I mixed honey with the water so that the body received some nourishment. The idea here was that during starvation the body itself draws reserve strength for the healing of injured organs. Sometimes I arranged a "nibbling": eating dried apricots, figs, and persimmon I brought from Central Asia. I took warm baths and began receiving massage therapy much earlier than the time selected by the doctors of the CSRA dispensary. I could feel that I was healing.

I went onto the ice two weeks or so earlier than is normal with such injuries.

There was a post script: In the summer of 1989 during a familiarization trip to Vancouver I underwent a very thorough medical examination, during which I told the club doctors about my ankle fracture a half-year earlier, and of my recovery.

"Please," they asked, "when you come for good in August with your family, write down in detail for us how it was done."

With an open attitude like that, they could never have worked at Archangel.

In retrospect, there was little I could have done to avoid Archangel. Had I gone to Spartak or stayed in Khimik I still faced the two years compulsory military service, and Tikhonov could simply have had me drafted and moved me to the CSRA. But one thing I knew: after those two years I would be gone. After that, the enslavement would end and I could live and play hockey where I wished.

Or so I thought.

After the first year, in which I achieved some world recognition and became a fixture on the National team's first line, my superior officers began to suggest that it would not be bad for me to "put on some epaulettes with stars". In other words, enter the officers' training program and extend my career in the military.

Oh, no.

"Thank you, of course, for the proposition," I said politely. "For now, living as a private is not bad. I'll go through my required two years, and then we will see."

We would see, all right. We'd see my back to Archangel.

The suggestions persisted. I continued to decline with thanks. They didn't want Igor the officer, who seldom even wore a military uniform; they wanted Igor the dispatcher, who trained with hockey sticks, not guns. And in one more year I would become a free man with choices: I could remain with CSRA by the right of signing again, but this time as a civilian playing on the team (there were two civilians on the CSRA club when I arrived; I believe in 1990 there are four or five). Small chance of that! Or I could go to Khimik or Spartak or any other club. Obviously, certain people were not prepared to wait around for my decision.

It was spring, and the CSRA had locked away the championship of the Soviet Union long before the schedule ended. But Tikhonov continued to pressure psychologically. We won every match, every single one of them and desirably by a large score. Nor did he allow even a little weakening of discipline: the National team. We must push ourselves ever harder to prepare for the National team competitions.

Then, without warning, he called me in.

"You know, Igor, we are playing Gorky," he said. "It is the last match. You can go home. Arrange some time off for yourself. Rest in Voskresensk, visit your parents. Just be back in time for the warm-up (the light exercise the morning of the match)."

"Good," I said, taken aback, but happy for the opportunity. "Thank you."

It never occurred to me that it was a tactical cover for his next move. But I soon found out. On the morning I returned from my unexpected holiday I was met by Tikhonov's assistant, Yuri Moiseev.

He shook my hand cordially.

"Welcome," he said, "You are now a lieutenant. An officer!"

A lieutenant? An officer? How could that be, I ask you, without my consent? But Moiseev laughed:

"Yes," he said jovially, "Quit getting excited! The order concerning conferring on you the lieutenant rank has already been signed!"

Not by me, it hadn't. Nor would it ever have been.

It was not a situation faced by me alone. It was, in fact, common practice. And not all other players so "honored" as "military" officers reacted so heatedly. They agreed – were thankful, probably. After all, future security was guaranteed: After the conclusion of the hockey career one would not have to think about earning one's daily bread, as do the majority of other sportsmen on other clubs.

All four of the Voskresensk members of the National club faced the same question. The variety of their responses is interesting.

Only recently I found out that when the CSRA started to use the same persuasions on Valeri Kamensky, to sign up as an officer, he rushed home to Voskresensk, to Khimik, and told everything as it was.

"What am I to do," he asked. "I'm being treated like some kind of traitor!"

And although Kamensky had already shone in Canada and had a place on the National team, no one risked advising him to refuse his prearranged "officer's stars". Would he not fall into disgrace with his majesty, Tikhonov? Could he not lose his place on the Nationals? So he was trapped, this talented forward, trapped with officer's stars he did not want.

Andrei Lomakin, the very same one whom I had led by the hand from the street into the section, bypassed the CSRA entirely, accepting instead an offer into Dynamo, also an army team but of another department. (He boastfully showed it in his native town, and does not show his face there any more. However, that's his personal affair).

And then there was Sasha Chernykh. On the youth national team he was regarded as the best centre, better even than Kamensky. When the CSRA took both of them, Kemensky moved up tremendously. But somehow Chernykh withdrew into the background. He didn't even make the base team of CSRA, modestly playing out his required two years somewhere in the backyards of the army provincial sports clubs. Then he returned to Voskresensk – and suddenly began to play as he knew how. He became a mainstay of the National team. Yet, in my opinion, he at best plays to 80 per cent of his potential.

And me? I was not taking it calmly enough to suit those who had entrapped me.

Even Moiseev's wife came to me – I understood at the urging of Tikhonov – to kindly explain at length (and also to hush up a possible scandal) that it was necessary and better that on the CSRA the hockey players be officers. The best hockey players in any case. And if a row was made, that would make things worse, and not only for me. And from the higher army levels they made me understand that I did not make up the rules and that I, a 20-year-old boy, could not change them.

I was an army lieutenant. Later I was promoted to captain – undoubtedly for battles won on the ice rinks of the world, for they were the only fields on which I ever fought for my country. But at whichever rank, the injustice of it never died within me. The rank I held rightfully belonged to a countryman who has been a soldier for two years and graduated from a military college. My uniform I wore perhaps twice a year, when the CSRA team was invited to the Ministry of Defence and the photographers scrambled to capture "Captain Larionov and his wife and daughter." We laughed at that among ourselves, but in that laughter there was no happiness.

Tikhonov was beaming, so happy at this completion of a successful operation that he freed our whole line from the morning exercise. "Rest, guys!" he said. Then he made us work anyway. It was not the first lie, nor the last.

Chapter 4
DARK ANGEL

I was sitting in the Olympic Village cafeteria in Sarajevo, wondering if for me the 1984 Olympic Games were over almost before they had begun. The night before, in an insignificant early-round match against Poland in the 1984 Olympic Games, I had severly strained a shoulder muscle. It is difficult to play this game when you cannot freely move one arm, and you cannot set a time on how long it will take to recover.

Suddenly, a well-known figure in Soviet hockey slid into the booth.

"What ever have you done?" he snapped. "How *could* you?"

I couldn't believe what I was hearing. He made it sound as though I'd gone out and injured myself on purpose.

"I collided with somebody," I said, somewhat unnecessarily. He'd been there. He'd seen it happen.

"So why do you think I brought you here?" he raved. "You let the whole team down!"

"Wait! Don't get excited," I said. "Maybe there is some way around it. I will win the tournament under anaesthesia!"

That's exactly how it happened. I played the rest of the tournament with the pain in my shoulder numbed by needles.

I will not stress the absurdity and inhumanity of that short conversation. It is self-evident. Hockey players are to blame when they receive injuries? Who could ever take that point of view? Only one man that I know of: the man who sat across from me in the booth.

Tikhonov. Viktor Vasilevich Tikhonov.

It is impossible to discuss Soviet hockey, its successes and its failures, without discussing in detail this man who for 14 years has been the absolute dictator in the selection and management of not one team, but two. For nine years I was under the charge of – or, more precisely, under the *press of,* this man "Tikanoff", as they pronounce his name abroad. I saw how his power was built, and found through experience how difficult, how next-to-impossible it was to overcome it. When finally I was free to try myself with the Vancouver Canucks, it was not Soviet hockey I was fleeing. As much as anything, it was Tikhonov.

To understand his power you must first understand the system under which it flourishes.

There are no wage negotiations in Soviet hockey. A player does not have an agent, does not negotiate the best deal he can and pick his team accordingly. There are no signing bonuses, no instant wealth. Everyone gets the same basic 350 rubles, the officers adding a little more as their Army rank improves. Once a player goes to a team, his dependence on his coaches is complete.

My country still has many economic problems to solve – problems that are a concern to the sportsman as much as to anyone else: a dwelling, a car, a cottage, furniture. And it is true that a famous hockey player will obtain these comforts more quickly than an ordinary worker, because the coach is interested in the strong defenceman or forward, and he tries to ensure that hockey players are not enticed to join another club because of these everyday matters. To such a degree do we depend upon the power of the senior coach and the opportunities he can present us that today's Soviet hockey player is almost in bondage.

And with this being the case for a man who coaches one team, how much is it magnified in the case of Tikhonov, who coaches two? In all developed hockey powers the senior coach of the national team is free from work in any other club. Otherwise subjectivism emerges, and abuse of one's position. But since 1977 Tikhonov has combined the incompatible – coaching both CSRA and the National team – and feels splendid about it!

"I have two teams to prepare in a year," he told Canadian reporters during one of our tours. "It's a big job. There are very few coaches in the NHL who could carry two teams each year."

True, it is a big job, a job that should be done by two men, not by one. And he accomplishes it at what cost to his players? For one thing, it becomes very difficult to maintain personal dignity, to live by one's principles, because this can give rise to conflicts with the coach, who will not fail to use your dependence on him while distributing his favors. And you, the player chaffing under such treatment, must keep remembering that at at home your wife and child wait for you, the breadwinner, whose living comes from the game this coach controls.

It is not a situation to encourage independent thinking. So I was reminded in conversation with Kasatonov during the autumn of 1984 as we shared a ride to Archangel with Volodia Zubkov. Even then my relations with Tikhonov were growing strained – not yet confrontational, but still not to be considered harmless. Due to an injury to Fetisov, Kasatonov was serving as temporary captain. As we drove, we got into a heated argument, an argument over principles.

"Hey, why do you argue all the time with Tikhonov, and swear at him?" Kasatonov asked me. "Igor, be a little smarter. In the end, do you need to remain in a one-room apartment? Don't you want to shine in front of your parents?"

"It doesn't matter what I need. I'm not asking for anything."

"But *I* need a three-room apartment. My child is growing up. Listen to my advice. When he calls you names, keep quiet! Let him call you names, let him do whatever he wants. But you, do your own thing, play. And that's all."

I could not understand such an attitude.

"Lesha, how can you speak that way?" I asked. "If I consider the coach to be wrong, why must I listen as he humiliates me in front of everybody? What am I, a man or a dumb robot?"

"Then *you,* old man, are wrong!" he replied. "Remember, you only have one life. And you have to do everything for your own sake. And all the rest is nonsense, it's not the main thing."

From that time on I ceased to relate to Alexei Kasatonov with trust. My friendship with him as an open and decent fellow, the one I had met 1981, drastically went downhill. I no longer considered him to be an individual. He was just another who had fallen into the trap of Tikhonov.

I have lived for almost 30 years, and I have not heard any reproach in my direction that I am not objective. There have been various periods in my life, serene and stormy, but with everything and everyone I have tried to judge from the position of facts, to judge fairly. I will try terribly to hold on to this rule in discussing this man who, because of his position, power and approach to the game, occupied such a particular place in my life.

I will not speak of the mass of impressions I amassed about our two-team coach. I will limit myself to the most essential. I will try to view Viktor Vasilevich Tikhonov from two towers, as a specialist and as a man.

In May of 1989, Makarov, Krutov, Vyacheslav Bykov and I took part in the new sports television programme "Arena." The conversation was sharp, having touched on the impending problems and recent conflicts. In the course of this talk around the round table, I named Tikhonov as a "talented coach." After that, friends and acquaintances who had seen "Arena" fell upon me: how could I make such compliments?

I want to be objective. There had been few of them, his pluses, but there were some.

He had been a defenceman and assistant coach with Moscow Dynamo when he was promoted to the senior position with the second-division Dynamo Riga in 1972. The team stood 14th when he took it. In his third year there it finished first and was promoted to the first division where it finished fourth in 1976, the year before Tikhonov was brought to Moscow to coach CSRA and the Nationals.

He brought with him from Riga the concept of using a fourth line, a total preoccupation with physical preparation, and an insane tempo which was in force for all three periods. This, too, he developed in Riga, where the team battled as if it were a matter of life and death, sometimes even beating the Moscow clubs. But for all that preparation, all the fanaticism, outstanding players did not come from Riga. Only Helmut Balderis is the exception.

And we won. But I ask again – at what price?

Tikhonov brought his "Rigian" system to the CSRA team, absolutely different than the traditional, both in writing and in composition. Anatoli Tarasov, the legendary National coach of earlier years, is known for his belief in encouraging creative individuality within the team system. He was a "player's coach", as they say in North America. It was Tarasov who found Valery Kharlomov outside the major structure of Soviet hockey, who recognized his individual mastery and brought him to the National team. And it was Tikhonov, with his structured system that utterly discouraged such individuality, who caused the magnificent masters, Kharlomov and Petrov, to become bewildered and disagreeable

To this day it is Tarasov, the blustery bear recently named as vice-president of the Soviet Ice Hockey Federation who is revered by the hockey fans as the father of the game in Russia, not the fanatical Tikhonov, who views victories as a personal triumph and defeat as the failure of players he himself had made good enough to win.

He did not spare himself, give him that. He worked, nights on end without sleep, watching video tapes of the matches, twisting them this way and that, analyzing them. You cannot take that away from him. I will not take away all the coaching talent of Tikhonov. By no means.

But the back side of the coin was his fanaticism. His was a constant round-the-clock hockey vigil. Every action was aimed and justified by his interpretation of the single aim: victory – everything, including his obviously inhumane conduct. I do not accept this in principle! And are there really coaches who do not wish to see their own underlings as victors? So much so that their endless references appear as worship to Tikhonov's fanaticism.

In NHL clubs the enormous range of the coach's functions are sensibly defined. Someone answers for the physical preparation of the team, and another for the tactical teaching. In our hockey this is not so.

Tikhonov: "Is the physical preparation in order? Your emotions interest me little!"

Viktor Valisevich records everything that is possible, forever writing in thick notebooks. This habit, too, he brought with him from Riga. And probably the thickest of these notes are concerned with the physical, the conditioning of the player. He supervises this aspect as one would take care of a child. I agree it is an important part of the preparation, but surely not to the repression of all else.

He is not a man who likes change in this area, preferring to stay with the system he has used for years to get his players into top shape. If it is not his way, it cannot be the right way.

Only once, in 1988, did he bend, and then it was but briefly.

We were standing on the tartan track under the scorching sun, awaiting with horror the inevitable run to exhaustion around the stadium. But no – unexpectedly they took the running program to Archangel. To me it seemed that Tikhonov had become a bit more lost, changing things while he searched. But in this instance, good. We could run in the country, through the forest in the country-clean air.

But we had not Tikhonov to thank for it. It was the idea of a sensible fellow, the scientist of the staff, Igor Zakharin. He suggested new ideas to the senior coach, without whose supervision perhaps only the cook on the base worked. He suggested more player exercises, games that would give some variety to the physical preparations without taking away from the effect. The players gladly took to the new games. We hoped that they would enter into our everyday training. We forgot that, under Tikhonov, to expect serious change was to look for a tropical heat wave in the dead of winter.

Zakharin phoned me at home and asked me to meet him. I was then immovable with a plaster cast on my right ankle, broken in a game Oct. 28, 1988, enjoying the luxury of not having to appear at the CSRA, and the pleasure of doing without the "ardent love and deep respect" of my coach.

I had known Igor Zakharin for about 13 years. He was from a city of the Volga region, Konakovo. As a boy he came to us in Khimik. We were together in a summer training camp. He was two years older than I was. Igor did not become a professional hockey player, he went into science. We saw him only in passing. He worked in Leningrad, but then moved to us in the CSRA (where, despite his abilities, he lasted only one year).

We spoke over tea in the kitchen.

"Openly, now," he asked me. "Do you and the guys like those things that I have introduced into the team's training?"

"Without question, old man," I assured him.

"Well then, tell me what to do! I worked out a whole method, a sensible training plan to get optimal results. I want to help you guys, but nothing is coming of it. Tikhonov won't change anything. He lives according to his own notebooks of 10 years past! If I stay on his team I am finished as a specialist. I'll be broken psychologically. And I have an interesting offer, to work for the Institute of Physical Culture, to head the faculty of hockey. Igor, what should I do?"

There was only one answer.

"Go," I told him. "I have already studied Tikhonov. It will be a pity not to have you with us, but go to the Institute."

Honor and praise for Igor Zakharin. He did not go with the current, did not bow before that all-powerful coach, did not work for the sake of foreign excursions. He has kept human dignity and a professional reputation. I have not met many such people.

Tikhonov: "I have had it with you. When I let you go for a night home, so then I have to sort it out. Break the regime, then it will take me 10 days to chase out the folly from you!"

It was the coach's running maxim: That we were such dishonest and irresponsible guys that, were we allowed to go home to our families and report to camp rather than live there, we would sit at the table with friends and put ourselves to hard drinking, and then our physical conditioning would come to such state that a long time was needed to bring us back to normal.

This was not in any way a touching concern for our health. It was a very convenient excuse to plant the team again under a long country arrest.

I do not get excited at the sight of cognac or vodka, wine or champagne. I control myself completely. In general I cannot touch a drop if I am not in the mood, or if it interferes with preparation for a match or tournament. I can sit with friends and control my drinking. My physical conditioning is my worry. And if the coach thinks that I have behaved myself improperly, that I am losing his physical conditioning, then I am the one who should be punished. Severely punished. I – not the whole team! To abuse or punish the whole team because of one or two who commit offences, only unleashes unhealthy passions and makes the situation on the team red hot.

Viktor Vasilevich loves very much to study this. This enters into his politics concerning the suppression of the hockey players as people in every way. His are the politics of a dictator: divide and rule.

Tikhonov: "I will send you all to the devil's mother! I will send you off to Moscow (if we are playing abroad). You have become completely insolent!"

Where and when did we hear this from the lips of the "great" coach? On the ice, during a game in which we were behind or not playing well. When the game was going well, he more or less held himself within the limits of decency. No wonder. But it was worth appearing under the team's cloud, if a little cloud, to literally break through the dam and stream of threats that was poured down everyday on our heads and on occasion to snap back at him with my own feelings. The coach's threat of defeat was demoralizing. The level of the match or of our rivals did not matter. This abuse could start on the fifth or 10th minute, when even the most pessimistic hockey player would not have thought to fall into despondency. The easy-going Vova Krutov could not understand it.

"Hey what is he exploding at us for?" he'd ask an assistant coach. "Calm him down. He doesn't have to be that way! What is he panicking for? The game has just begun."

It was in the locker room after the first period that the very real hysterics of the coach began. We who were a little more experienced tried to bring him to reason:

"It would be better if you spoke more calmly, about what to do and how to play," we'd suggest. But he did not listen and did not hear.

"Do what you have to," he'd reply. "But win the match." Imagine, a coach saying that. A senior coach who is supposed to be making the adjustments, preparing us for the next period. It is absurd! And if after such "valuable" instructions the team began to play better, then Tikhonov would attribute the merit to himself.

To me, his conduct during the game, no matter what the situation, good or bad, is one of the main merits of a coach. Or, his enormous lacking.

Tikhonov: "You have to win every match by the highest score possible."

In general, as a strategist Tikhonov is good for nothing. In his dazzling thirst to win, to win, to win, he squeezes the last juice from the players, even when it is possible to win at half strength. He incorrectly estimated the strengths of the team. He worried little about our emotional reserves. In fact, he had but one worry: to announce to his superiors yet another success of the team, and thus the success, above all, of the coach.

Even when he was caught in gross errors in judgment he attempted to turn them to his own advantage so he would not appear to be in the wrong.

In world championships and the Canada Cup series, pacing is all-important. You must time things to be at your best in the big matches, particularly against Canada. But Tikhonov never could see this. So, when we lost the Canada Cup in 1984 and the world championship in 1985 and journalists asked him why he did not rest his stars, the KLM line, in the early games against weaker teams like Poland where 10-goal victories were not uncommon, his reply was that we always had to play to the maximum, to play every game to the limit. The message was clear: We had lost in the end, but he, Tikhonov, had not been in the wrong to do this.

Three years later we played in the Izvestia tournament and lost to the Canadians. Then we went to Calgary, and in a pre-Olympic exhibition lost to them again. And in the early Olympic games we were not beating the weaker teams by as great a margin as usual. But we did come on to capture the gold. And what did Tikhonov say then? He said that we had to lose the early games in order to be ready for the big ones. Suddenly, the great coach had discovered this great strategy! Again, came the impression, the credit for the gold medal must go to him! Amazing.

Had he bothered to ask the players, we might have given him this great strategy years earlier. But he was not one to approach players individually. At least, in eight years I do not once remember it happening. He was Tikhonov. He was king.

Abroad, the style of play of our line was called the "transition game." I found out about this only recently. Our game came together thanks to the abilities of everyone of our line, and the common striving to leadership and beautiful hockey. The coach, of course, brought us together and complemented the squad, you cannot take that away from him. But no kind of special tactical assignments or exercises of the first line were made.

Our squad, independent of the coach's instructions, planned our approach to a game on the bench before going out on the ice. We corrected the coach's assignments for a particular situation. We changed tactics "on the fly". Without all of this it would have hardly been possible to show hockey of such a high class for almost 10 years in a row. But you will not hear that from Tikhonov.

Yes, we five always felt ourselves as leaders, and always tried to lead. Almost always, in my opinion, we were successful. We consciously loaded on ourselves higher burdens, gladly put out on the ice when our team was on the power play, or in defending short-handed. However much this happened through the game, particularly in the Soviet Union, when it was possible for us to appear a little more sharp, it was as if the coach did not notice.

You would think that in club tournaments like the IZVESTIA, he would logically leave us alone and concentrate on the new players, the candidates for the National team. But no. Apparently, he got used to having us at hand like a magic wand, and the rest did not worry him.He got lucky with us. He put together a line, and it worked from the beginning. He did not change anyone, he did not shuffle us. How would you call it? He hit the bull's eye with the first shot.

But again, how difficult was it to assemble us? At the level we were playing, he could scarcely avoid noticing us. "Filya" Fetisov was already a player, a huge player! Mikhailich, as I call Makarov, was already rated a gifted winger. Without them the first line would not have been possible with any sort of magician.

With Kasatonov, Krutov and myself, the situation for the coach was somewhat different. We were younger, and had played less as masters.

He took Krutov immediately to the Olympics, and he played there well. With time it became a Tikhonov habit: to every important tournament, take a rookie. I do not know where he got this characteristic. He took greenhorns, and these people were immediately put to use and written into the team. There was something in this. This was a coaching originality, a risky move he took many times.

Before this I would not name Tikhonov as a "risky" coach. It was entirely the other way around. Invitations to rookies were more the exception than the rule. He was lucky with our line. It is possible to see a good player with an untrained eye – but to take an average player and to make an outstanding hockey player of him, this is, really, a risk.

Tikhonov: "If I would have been given this team, I would not lose ever to anyone!"

Tikhonov made this statement at the press conference at Rendez-Vous '87. Krutov was there for the team and heard him say it. By one of these boastful, unsound phrases "Tikhonoff" showed his personal immodesty and humiliated our team. Our team, that he coached! He made us appear a useless little team that under the wise leadership of Tikhonov was able to beat any team, such as the Canadians. The terrifying thing is that, in his mania, he believes it. Viktor Vasilevich Tikhonov is convinced: He and only he is in reality able to prepare the players.

I do not remember it literally, but I remember the thought expressed by him after Krutov was acknowledged as the best hockey player in the world for 1987. He loudly announced that Krutov shone exceptionally so because he, Tikhonov, had prepared him like a trainer for all of two weeks. For me, such an announcement was simply enraging. It had nothing in common with reality.

December 1988. Critical days for me. I was rehabilitating after an ankle fracture. It was two months since my article appeared in OGONYOK, Tikhonov craved vengeance, and he had a beautiful opportunity for it.

I did not train with the big team. My leg was still throbbing. But I told everyone, my doctor first of all, that every thing was okay. Logically it was worth it to me to show the coach that there should be no doubt about taking me to the IZVESTIA tournament, and then to Canada for the NHL Super Series. But I had misgivings. I knew that in addition to his usual vengefulness, there would be his conviction that only he, Tikhonov, was able to prepare a hockey player.

It is not particularly surprising that Tikhonov is as he is. His human shortcomings fell in the fertile soil of absolute power and absolute permission to do things. They served only to strengthen the negative aspects of his character.

The cult of Tikhonov was established. A very real cult of personality. Soviet hockey suffered seriously for it. Through the years it was drummed into the heads of the coaches, players and yes, even the fans, that there was only one great hockey specialist in the country: Tikhonov. And no matter how regrettable this is, many people continually came to believe in this demagoguery. Not only hockey players themselves, but those who played coaching politics, who used his methods and parroted his philosophies to save their own skins.

A coach. How can one evaluate a person in this most interesting profession? Talented toiler, psychologist, teacher, theoretician, tactician... all of these things he must be in varying degrees, and more.

How would I evaluate Tikhonov? I cannot immediately define him.

I cannot doubt his services in certain areas. Tikhonov strived to resolve everything himself. His hands were unfettered, and as a coach he could do absolutely everything that was combined as necessary for the club or the National team. He broke through problems – problems every coach had – in the offices of superiors. Not everyone knew how to do this, for it demanded a particular talent. But with that talent our senior coach was strengthened and even without it exercised an enormous power over us hockey players.

He knew how to place himself on top, in the CSRA, in Goskomsport, the governing body of all Soviet sport, so that they gave him unlimited power. He knew how to use that time, those structures, to bring the team together, and with that team to win. He knew how to select people for the team, although it was not that complicated when everything was under his hands, when he had unlimited opportunity.

I started out to separate Tikhonov the coach and Tikhonov the person. But that is too artificial a division. It is possible to be a splendid coach-psychologist, or coach-theoretician, or coach-tactician, but if it is not combined with principles, then no amount of talent or work will save it.

The mastery of coaching is working with people. With people! That is with the young, who spend the best part of their hockey life under his management. The coach commands dignity, but he does not have the right to treat the hockey players like pigs.

The merits of Tikhonov prior to hockey, which there are and which I partially admit, do not make up for the way he treated subordinates. For his dishonesty. For the many humiliations and insults to his players regarding their worthiness, which occurred almost every day. Many do not know this. But, we players did not throw this from our memory. From us, there is nowhere he can hide it.

Tikhonov: "Your line is simply a superstructure. If I put you all on the bench, the team would get long splendidly without you!"

Or:

"Yes, I will get rid of you all, then I will find me some stars!"

Or:

"No one is irreplaceable!"

Through the years we, who have been acknowledged in the world as leaders, tolerated similar outcries, many accompanied – particularly in the heated tension of a match – by unprintable expressions. We suffered, grinding our teeth, in exasperation, as insults burned in us. I grew disgusted with the coach.

In the clubs of the NHL, the division of duties of the coaches is clearly defined. But we had a coach who was the head of everything! Usually our specialists lament that they are required to be occupied by all the questions, which are not entirely connected with hockey: finding a hockey player's apartment; helping him get a car, furniture and other material necessities; even the dacha (summer cottage) that is like a gift from the sky, particularly when you have not even dreamed of it. I am prepared to sympathize with several coaches. However, in Tikhonov's case this concentration of power could not have come at a better time. He has used it like a weapon. It has helped to carry through his own policies, to frighten or to lure, but in principle to keep the players tied down. If he wants someone, he will give them a present. If he wants to ruin someone, he will rub salt in, under any pretence.

Viktor Vasilevich has a diehard system, but in some things he shows visible leniency.

For a breaking of curfew at the training camp, he punished Krutov by excluding him from an exhibition tournament in Switzerland. Because the national team draws huge crowds abroad, players earn about $600 for these meaningless matches. Thus. he punished his family materially. However, he would not do this to a player before an *important* tournament. No. In that situation he would not lose such a splendid winger; not for anything in the world! Here he forgives everything.

One young defenceman of the CSRA during an appearance abroad broke the rules of conduct in a supermarket and was thrown out by a security guard. Tikhonov could have made a fuss, but it could have cost him the defenceman. How did he conduct himself? He quickly settled everything and hushed up a possible scandal.

Tikhonov presents himself as a man of principles. But if he was so severe and principled, then Alexander Mogilny would not have been available to help win the world junior championship in 1989.

He'd been given a 10-game suspension for a fight in the spring match of the championship of the USSR. But the talented and honorable Mogilny was needed for a National team, and Viktor Vasilevich momentarily forgot about the fight.

For Tikhonov in the end there is only one principle: that everything should be good for him.

And he had another weapon, a weapon so despicable it is difficult to discuss. Tikhonov had a spy.

We had lost a game, and in the dressing room the passions had not yet cooled. We conducted an operative analysis of the game: we praised one another, criticized, said what we felt had to be said, and discussed how we had lost as a team. And we cursed the coach in his absence for what we considered his poor instructions. But this was a gentlemanly discussion, a conversation behind closed doors in which the early emotions ran high. It was supposed to begin and end there.

The next morning, during the team meeting, it became apparent that Tikhonov was well posted on what the players had said in our private discussion.

How could this be? There is a name for it: informing. There was an informer, or informers, on our team.

It left a disgusting feeling, knowing that people – teammates! – making common talk with you were not honest. Someone looks at you with clear eyes, saying yes to your comments, saying something themselves, and then...

The information was not received by the head coach, reacted upon and forgotten. Oh, no. Each item was carefully written down and kept on file for possible future use in discrediting a player. Compromising material, it is called, a link to the spirit of the worst times from the history of our country.

Tikhonov: "So I will take it, and talk a bit about your prank, that you created. I will find something like this on every one, so that people will be amazed. And you will have to pay for it."

This is known as keeping a person on the hook: you dare lift your head, so I will drown you in an instant, I will take from your dossier something compromising to you.

In May of 1989, after the World Championship, after the end of the season filled with conflict, when Fetisov and I openly, in the press, confronted Tikhonov with sufficiently serious claims which he persistently refused to answer publicly, Viktor Vasilevich

57

suddenly pulled out at the meeting of the Hockey Federation of the USSR the long concealed compromising material.

"Yes, I have such material in relation to Fetisov and Larionov, that it threatens them with a prison sentence of six to eight years!"

This was made public in the press.

But Vacheslav and I launched a newspaper counter-attack:

"The covering up of such material opposes legislation. We categorically demand these documents be made public. We protest against the application of a system of collection of compromising material by Tikhonov as anti-educational and anti-democratic.

"Unfortunately, this complied with the perpetual policies of Tikhonov in relation with sportsmen. The compromise against Fetisov emerged by a similar way in the "Kiev" affair. After the time of our work with comrade Tikhonov, all relations with disagreement he built, blackmailing them as if he had compromising material on them.

"We consider such relations with people unworthy in a democratic state. This is seen as an anarchism of Stalinist times."

I knew what kind of stone the coach held behind his back these years. I knew it not for a rock, but for a pebble.

It was 1985, and I was driving calmly down the Ilinsk highway leading to Archangel. I was about a kilometre from the base when, out of nowhere, a man seemed almost to throw himself under the wheels of my Zhiguli. I slammed the brake pedal, but the distance was too short. I felt a thump. When the ambulance came to take the injured man away, the attendants said he was in a state of extreme drunkenness.

When word of the accident reached the team, Tikhonov naturally decided that I had been in the wrong. Moreover, since I had attended the funeral of my grandmother that morning, and the commemoration gathering that followed, he did not doubt that I was far from sober.

The workers of GAI (Government Auto Inspection) maintained a different opinion. They took me to the nearest branch, where they took my pulse and blood pressure. So sure were they that I had not had even a drop of alcohol that they did not even take a sample of blood for analysis. The affair of the road accident was closed. I was blameless.

It is true that Tikhonov fussed and endeavored to get things settled calmly and quickly. I was, remember, on the first line, and that must not be altered. But now, reaching into his archives for something to hold against me as a threat, he was acting as though he had pulled me from great trouble, saved me from prison. Yes – in this incident where I had been proved blameless!

But in the end, after Fetisov's and my protest in the newspaper, he did not publish it. This, then, was the coach who commanded me for eight years.

I remember when the Petrov line left hockey. Now it was our turn – Fetisov, Makarov, Krutov and I, all in one go, trailed by threats and insults to human dignity. Instead of warm and respectful farewell and mutual gratitude at the conclusion of many years of mutual work, a complete break. It was both sad and unnecessary.

I don't know of one man who ever left Tikhonov's CSRA or the National team under good terms. (Well, Kasatonov perhaps, later). For there was one missing space on the coaching certificate of Victor Vasilevich: Nowhere had he ever learned how to deal with people. It was a loss for both sides.

Chapter 5
KLM

The game of hockey is not simple. It is not, as it can appear to those seeing it for the first time – or, for that matter, many times – five men attempting to put the puck in a rival's net and joining a sixth to prevent the rivals from putting it in yours. Without mutual understanding and compatibility among the five, there is nothing.

Our sport is not alone in this need. Soccer, basketball, handball, water polo also require this need for a group to perform as one. But for all the players to decide instantaneously, to understand each other instantaneously and execute manoeuvres instantaneously; for the squad, the whole five to be as the fingers in one clenched fist? Only in hockey!

And because of that dependency, any break, any lessening in that mutual understanding, in that oneness, you inevitably turn sour and cannot perform to even half your strength. The players sense it happening. Some become annoyed or desperate, seeking out other linemates better suited to their skills, who would welcome them as they themselves would be welcomed. As a nice girl dreams of a handsome fiance, so do hockey players cherish the dream that at some time they will fall into the company with such fellows, with whom they will know how to forge together "the" squad, a deserving squad in which everyone on the line will blossom. To find it is to find the six-figure number in the sports lottery.

I drew the lucky ticket.

I fell in with a squad that for eight years in succession was held up by the world as an example, as the very best. I was the last to arrive, the final piece of the puzzle, and it was as though I had jumped on a departing train. A train departing into a happy distance.

After the war years when "Canadian" hockey appeared in the USSR, our coaches attached enormous meaning to the permanent search for striking squads. There may not have been a search to equal it at any time in any hockey nation.

At first, the players with the combination of talents to form such squads appeared very rarely. When this small miracle happened, two major problems were solved immediately: the playing of these lucky ones became the hockey fashion, examples to be imitated. For these men, though, all peace ended, because it was now up to them to decide the outcome of the decisive competitions. And they, as a rule, would manage with the entrusted mission.

Traditionally, our lines are named after the centre. And we had our famous ones known to every schoolboy. The Bobrov Line, the Almetov Line, the Starshinov, Polupanov, Shadrin and Petrov. I remember well the Shadrin line. I dreamed of being like Volodia Shadrin, who was the "center" of a faultless breakaway attack. I can still see in front of my eyes the Petrov line, which improvised well.

In general, I assume that without the ability for unexpected movement, the squads did not become first lines. But, according to the words of the coaches of the senior generation, our line has distinguished itself at a level higher than achieved by masters in the past.

Heady praise, indeed – and for me, it could so easily have gone another way.

When Tikhonov came to Voskresensk to lure me to the CSRA for the 1981-82 season, he was looking for a playmaker, a centre who could make things happen. He had Makarov and Krutov, but as wingers he found them no more menacing than the team of Helmut Baldaris and Sergei Kapustin. In fact, he had it in his mind to put me between the latter two, but by that time they had been split. That left him with a problem: He had me. Now what was he to do with me? Put me between Makarov and Krutov on the first line, or on another line he was in the process of forming?

In fact, he told journalists later, he had another in mind for the centre role on the first line."I will not hide it," he told them. "There were still doubts about this Voskresensk lad."

The doubts centred not around my ability, but my size and strength. "Igor did not possess sufficient physical conditioning for higher levels. (But) I was not wrong (in selecting him). Only from appearance does he seem to be so thin, so fragile, but the very thing is that this is a very strong fellow. During the years of being in the CSRA, he has gained strength."

In the end, he decided to try me on the first line. And – or so he claimed – he knew from the start, on that very day ("Perhaps I, alone.") that he had a real first squad.

"Igor was, as they call it, in his own place," he told the journalists. "Immediately finding a common language with the wingers. That humdrum day with the morning calisthenics and two two-hour training sessions became for me, for them, for us all, a holiday. We came to properly value it only later. I had a line, a talented line to play contemporary hockey. And how they could play!"

Makarov, Larionov, Krutov, Kasatonov, Fetisov. Yes, we could play. For nine years, on the world stage, we played as one, strived as one and – on the ice at least – thought as one. We began in September, 1981 and finished in May, 1989 and played – how many games?

Let's see: the training games during the summer do not count. For the championship of the Soviet Union, 50. International matches in the course of the season for the club, approximately 15. And for the National select team, including world championships, certainly 20. How many do we have? Eighty-five matches in a year – five more than an NHL team's regular schedule, probably a total equal to theirs counting their training exhibitions.

Eighty-five multiplied by nine seasons equals 765 games. To make it a round number, 750! It is unlikely that this number is too high, especially considering that Tikhonov did not give us a break, even when there was not a threat.

It mattered not whether our team was outplaying our rivals or being outplayed, or whether the tempo was fluctuating, or even worse yet, whether the team was losing and time was running out before the final buzzer. It was "Let's go Greens!" And we Greens, so called because of the sweaters we wore during training, would jump over the boards to save our team.

In general, the squad used to be overworked, but we also had plenty of opportunities to shine, more opportunities than others. And, if we are to be objective, we played longer than the rest. There are partners who have played together longer, on other CSRA squads or select teams. But on the first squad? No.

Our line rolled out onto the ice for 750 matches! It becomes a little eerie even for me, such an impressive number.

Play the videotapes of the matches played by us in slow motion and you'd probably note an interesting detail: there were matches – not many of them, but some – where the strongest line in the world, the Greens, did not show any clear superiority over their competitors. This could be seen happening during the always prestigious Canadian tournament, and in the friendly meetings with the national teams of Finland, Sweden, or Czechoslovakia, and also in the scheduled matches for the All-Union championships with Khimik, Dynamo, or Soviet Wings.

Play those videotapes objectively, this way and that way, in slow or fast forward, and you will not see any evident superiority. But see also that in nine out of 10, when our game was not going well or the competition was worthy, the team won all the same.

Coincidence? It was repeated quite often. Luck? Perhaps, but they have been saying from the ancient times concerning sports: the strong also have luck. To me it is all too simple to think that if you are the strongest you should not have any difficulties and get everything on a silver platter.

We were really concerned about our own reputation. The mark of the team! Should we, God forbid, lose our innersquad game, everyone took it almost as a personal insult. It warped our collective dignity. The ambition of our squad was, I admit it, simply colossal! And that is why we devoted just a little more strength and emotion than had our competitor. And here probably lies the source of our "luck."

I did not see my arrival at the CSRA in quite the same viewpoint as Tikhonov. Realistically, I had two serious arguments for optimism: In the youth and youngster levels I had been regarded among the best in the country. And meeting face-to-face with foreign players of the same age, I did not bring shame on the squad. But another thing I could not forget: after the youth tournament in which I was named the outstanding player, Krutov, not I, had been asked to the Olympic Games team.

It had been like a hot and cold shower, the move from nowhere of note, widely known only to hockey fans in Voskresensk, to the "rejection" by the selectors for the Olympic side. And now, the move from a small town and a club that, despite its solid reputation for many years, was not brilliant at the time, to the big city and CSRA, the long-time ruler of the whole Soviet arena. I was attempting to join the likes of Valeri Kharlamov (who died two months later in a car accident), of Vladimir Petrov and Boris Mikhailov and Vladislav Tretiak.

I knew that such an invitation amounted to a 90 per cent chance of winning a place on the National team. But I, too, had reservations about my build. I felt I lacked sufficient strength, endurance and energy to give all throughout an entire game or tournament. Yet, any somewhat trained specialist can help you draw on your inner reserves and reach your maximum. I decided to kill two birds with one stone: increase my strength while maintaining my light weight and thus my manoeuvrability. Meanwhile, be sharp around the goal, Igor! Avoid the big guys!

But, for all that, a third element was needed if I was to survive: Partners! Partners! Those guys who with their mastery and character would compliment each other and me, to help me rise to full height. I needed partners like I need oxygen. Because to be in a class squad is equal to living in an ecologically clean city – a city where every corner, every house is dear to you, where every day is not wasted.

I came to this temple of hockey with an unconscious sharpness to my spyglass, examining closely these people with whom I was destined to go through thick and thin. The first few days would be important. Some I knew in passing, some from hearsay. Most of them already had a heady list of accomplishments. How would they receive me? How would my acclimatization go to the high altitudes? I made one decision immediately. I would not ingratiate myself with anybody. I would remain as I was.

My frame of mind then was defined by first impressions of the four main players – Krutov and Fetisov, who had come up through the CSRA, and the other two "outsiders" invited from other cities, Makarov from Chelyabinsk and Kasatonov from Leningrad. With the passing whirling years, some impressions of these masters would be proven wholly true, some would change for the better and some for the worse, and some would prove to have been false altogether.

"Krut."

Sometimes it seems Vladimir Krutov and I have always been together despite the times apart when we retreated to our club teams – me to Voskresensk, he to CSRA – after playing as linemates in the youngster and youth National tournaments. In Russia to get to know someone very well is called "eating the whole pod of salt". Well, if not the whole 36 pounds, Vova and I together ate half a pod each.

Through it all – the childhood matches, the nine years on the National team and now the journey to the Canucks and the NHL – we shared everything: arguments until hoarse, injuries and bruises, playing beyond our abilities, pregame jitters, the higher responsibility for the deeds of the squad, the joy of victories. There was no distrust, envy or alienation between us. There was human contact. Direct and open, with a frank soul. He has been able to keep all these character traits as a mature sportsman. You could not find such a master and competitor, or a more sincere, honest fellow.

We were street urchins together in, of all places, Voskresensk, at an all-Soviet tournament involving teams from Penza, Chelyabinsk, Riga, and of course, the CSRA and Spartak from Moscow. He was still not clearly the best, but stood out because he was good and quick, even if he was a little chubby. He understood the goings on well on the ice, he scored a lot, and he crawled into the very depths of hell, not sparing himself. He had a nickname, Pupsik: being small, but with a large head and such chubby limbs, with rosy cheeks, broken in and not at all thin, not like I a skeleton! Immediately he called forth a feeling of fondness in me for him, as a player and as a person.

The second time we happened to be together was on the youngster National teams. We quickly and forever became friends. I liked his unsophistication and kindness. We almost won it all, although at this age the battles are more reckless than with adults. Even then, we shared the feeling of leadership, the feeling of being unbeatable.

There were a couple of incidents we both remember.

In the 1977-78 European youth championship final we went almost five periods against Finland. Midway in the match a puck tipped off someone's stick and hit him squarely in the face. He fell to the ice, groggy, then got up and skated toward the bench and the doctor. Unfortunately, this gave the Finns a temporary numerical advantage, and they used it well to score.

Our coach criticized him sharply. He should not have left the ice until a player change! Despite the pain, he had no *right* to exclude himself from the play in such a way, not for anything! Vladimir was crushed. Never before – or since – had anyone questioned his guts. He was standing there on the ice, his stitches barely in, when I put my arm on his shoulder.

"Don't let it get to you," I said. "Rest. Then we'll build a merry-go-round for them! We'll get it back."

And we did, only to lose 6-5 in that second overtime to a goal by Jari Kurri.

A year later in the final of the world youth tournament we met the Finns again, with players like Kurri and Reijo Ruotsalinen, who would both later star in the NHL. And, as luck would have it, the leftwinger on our line, Vladimir Golovkov, had suffered a concussion on the eve of the match. We were in serious trouble. Krutov and myself, considering ourselves the leaders, felt we had to find an answer.

In the evening, when the coaches were wracking their brains trying to figure how to reassemble the lines, we went to their room and asked them to do nothing.

"Put Golovkov out on the ice as normal," we urged them. "Let him skate around somehow, but we'll work for him and no one will guess his condition."

We were able to keep our word. We won the match and the championship, 2-1.

Thus, as I came to CSRA, I knew I had one friend waiting for me, one comrade-in-arms from seasons past who had seven years' experience in that club at various levels. I would need help, support in word and deed. Instinctively, I probably waited for his supportive shoulder.

It did not turn out that way. That is, there was an elementary attention shown, he was warm, but nothing more. I was not offended. Vladimir himself had yet to occupy a firm position on the team, or come to exercise great authority. He had his own game to play. But I knew – and I was not ever wrong – that when I truly needed him, he would be there.

"Filya,"

A few days after his 20th birthday, Viacheslav Fetisov received a prize as the best defenceman at the 1978 World championships. In my opinion, his calibre has not yet been equalled.

"Filya", with his enormous talent and his remarkable character, was for me an idol. The first time Slava and I associated with each other was at the Olympic base in Staiki, near Minsk. From afar I'd had the impression that earlier glory had made him slightly arrogant – inevitable, perhaps, at 20, but like a children's illness, something better had, recovered from, and forgotten. Meeting him, I saw that his giddiness did not appear to last long.

We sat in a bar at the sports base, unhurriedly sipping on orange juice, talking about the life of a hockey player. Or rather, Fetisov talked and I listened more and made a note of it. Up close, he appeared a different person. Kind, and very anxious about the common good.

He did not carry himself arrogantly, yet at that moment the distance between us was tremendous. In men's hockey, I had not yet totally proven myself. Then, as I began to feel at home in the CSRA, I sensed him supporting and keeping a watchful eye on me. There was a sharpness to his character, an unpredictablity. An acknowledged innovator of the game of the contemporary defence-man, he could not be entirely virtuous, and could not behave himself among people as if on a memorized plan.

This is all a trifle. A year or two later we were considered equals, but the esteem and inner respect I had experienced for him as a youth remained with me. He was and is a creative personality, prepared to take a risk in the game for the sake of a result or for beauty. Fetisov was always the real leader of our line. He solidified it. There was not a single time when he faltered in a difficult moment! Always he supported, rescued and strengthened.

The two of us loved to stay on the ice after practice. The others would be splashing in the showers and we'd be out there thinking out every possible play situation. What would happen if I gave him a pass and he risked breaking it open and going into the attack? Krutov would back him up, Makarov would speed for insurance to the far goalpost, and Kasatonov would undertake a distractive manoeuvre. Or what if...?In nine years we played a lot of "What if...? And no one played it better than he.

"Sergei"

The opinion that I had formed about Fetisov was very important, for it was clear that Viacheslav would define the climate of the CSRA and even of the national team. However, the figure of Sergei Makarov, a player almost as distinguished as Fetisov, worried me no less. And if I knew Krutov, the leftwinger, inside and out, then Makarov, the partner on the right, remained for me a riddle even after my inclusion into the CSRA.

He was two years older than me, an inch shorter but 10 pounds heavier – hot-tempered and, like Krutov, not willing to tolerate clearly unjust calls or, in particular, low acts by rivals. Against them, he immediately tried to settle accounts. But what a player! In 1980 he'd won the Golden Stick award as the best player in Europe, and had played another year with the National team after that.

Strictly speaking, Sergei and I got to know each other earlier. In the spring of 1981 they took me to a tournament in Sweden – and left me without anything to do. They still had Vladimir Petrov with them as dispatcher, and I was a kind of spare, or something. I trained by myself in my own way. No one in particular had any expectations from me, and uncertainty does not create the best conditions for a stiff upper lip.

But I played out several matches with Makarov and Krutov. At once the feeling rose within me that I could not lose with these fellows. But immediately I did not know how to crack Sergei.

When he was in a bad mood, he locked himself in a shell. He had his own understanding of life and hockey, which he held to firmly and revealed rarely. All this I understood considerably better later. But then what? Makarov was already performing solo on the ice. He was brilliant! He maintained a neutral relationship towards me, quite reserved. He took care not to show any favoritism, but also did not shut me out. Apparently, he recognized in me a professional, and therefore was patient with me when some things did not go completely smoothly in the beginning. For this I was grateful to him.

With Makarov, I did not immediately choose a line of behavior. I understood intuitively that one should not dig into his soul, to pull at him, that it was better for us both to maintain amicable businesslike conditions. And I guessed right! For all these years, Sergei supported the squad somewhat separately, but I do not remember that he ever let it down, or that he disappointed us as a human being.

"Kasik"

And the last one from that company, whom I joined in the best years of my sports life, is "Kasik", Alexei Kasatonov, a robust fellow, 6'1" and 210 pounds, with ruddy cheeks and such recklessness in the eyes.

He is from Leningrad. For some reason unknown to me, they do not produce class hockey masters there in the "Northern Venice." But sometimes gifted guys appear on the banks of the Neva, and Kasatonov was one such fellow. Not quite original, yet he was not without talents. On the Leningrad team, almost without doubt, he would have stopped growing, and then would have dwindled all the more, because he had not gone along with a strict sports regime when it came to alcohol.

But he corrected himself in time, and when our squad was formed it seemed as if Kasatonov had grown two heads above himself. He has improved that much in his hockey mastery. With Lesha I had no problem in establishing contact. As it usually happens among such giants, he distinguished himself by kindness, sympathy and spinelessness. He very easily gave in to someone else's influence. For good or for bad, this is how he was – not able, it seemed, to quite grasp everything at once.

From the beginning, he was a staunch supporter of Viktor Tikhonov. He did not at first see me as a potential first-line player ("an ugly duckling," he saw me in the early days). And when I made it, he gave the credit where he thought it was due – to Tikhonov. As he saw it, the senior coach fought for me, to get me from Khimik, when others might have given up. And he fought for him, Kasatonov, despite his drinking and recklessness, waiting through the entire first season when he did not immediately show his best. All of these things, he said, pointed to Viktor Vasilevich as a great coach.

Ah, well. It would not do if we all agreed on every matter. And opinions do change, as my impressions of the first days, and even the first years of Kasatonov, unfortunately, had to be seriously corrected afterwards. And frankly I will say, not for the better. But, more about this later.

The Greens were not only colleagues according to the profession and likemindedness in hockey, not only of the same club and even not only players of one squad We were also friends. Each one had his own circle of friends and relatives and others close to their hearts. But the partners of the squad were always happy to see each other during nonworking hours.

One would think that the neverending stay at the country base, and in training, our touring over the whole of the enormous country and the world, would have left a fervent desire to be away from one another. Nothing of the kind happened. We lived so easily together, there was such enthusiasm, such happiness at the play and, of course, the results: victory after victory. We'd be gathered somewhere, a restaurant, perhaps, or another's home, sincerely trying to divert from the subject of hockey, a topic that held little interest among the girlfriends. And then someone would let slip something about the play of our squad, and in a moment we'd be caught in a chain reaction, discussing previous mistakes, thinking up new combinations. All but hockey was instantly forgotten as we plunged into our business and our love. I am not sure that such an inseparableness is necessary for a class squad. But for us it lasted five years.

And so, I have told you about my own partners. Partners one could only have dreamed about. I had joined a line that within *two months* would come to be known to the whole world as the Larionov line. All of us were completely unlike the others, but united by a love of hockey and blessed by nature with the abilities to play it at a high level.

The power and strength of our line could never be evaluated according to primitive arithmetic addition: the innovation and steadfastness of Fetisov, plus the reliability and self-sacrifice of Kasatonov, plus the elegance and refinement of Makarov, plus the fearlessness and pressure of Krutov, plus the dispatcher disposition of Larionov. No, no, as long as we were together and we had the same intentions, the line was transformed into a force far stronger than that which you would get by adding up our merits and abilities. It was a joyful, undeniable fact: The Greens were made for each other.

The first test for the Greens was more or less at the Canada Cup 1981. The only tournament where all the best of world hockey were gathered. As a line we were unknown, even to compatriots. And contrary to the Russian saying, the first potato pancake was not spoiled. We played, maybe not completely brilliantly, not so to make our rivals think only how to deal with us. This would begin approximately half a year later. However, it was evident even to the dilettante, that he was witnessing the debut of a new force in world hockey.

We had one special edge: our youth. Each of us could be considered at the beginning of his journey. Logically, we could only get stronger. Anatoli Vladimirovich Tarasov, a patriarch of Soviet hockey and an authority world renowned, wrote in the newspaper after the Canada Cup: "We have never before had such a marvellous squad. Just imagine their combined age is only 108 years!" The prognosis of Tarasov proved to be true.

Journalists charged with selecting the symbolic all-world team have an unwritten rule: they chose players from as many countries as possible. But in 1983 in West Germany they chose our whole line. Even Petrov's line with the legendary Kharlamov never achieved such an honor. And in 1986, in Moscow, history repeated. The world selects were Fetisov (USSR), Kasatonov (USSR), Makarov (USSR), Larionov (USSR), Krutov (USSR).I mention the AllStars not for the sake of praise, but to conclude: if journalists of various countries and publications, of various tastes and views of the game unanimously singled out our line, it means we brought a new word to the most popular game, brought in something of our own. Otherwise we would not for anything have been able to remain on the summit for so long.

Ah, I am starting to blow my own horn. All the same I will risk a comparison of my own: The Dutch had the total soccer mentality. We had total hockey. And we really should have the right to consider this a new page in the game. But what made it so?

I say improvisation. That is the word upon which we five built our play. Fetisov often compared it to music. "To me, improvisation for a hockey player is the same as for a jazz musician," he said. "But for the whole line to improvise, it is possible only when every player is strong, well versed in his tactical scope and rich in technical repertoire, when all together they understand one another with half a word and half a glance and even without one or the other, when to everyone it seems tedious to move only according to the plan of the hockey textbook, as we say, in the groove."

Again a comparison with soccer suggests itself. I think that there is more thought and more spirit, more of everything, on ice. I have played both games, one at the high level, the other at the very lowest. There is improvisation in soccer, but it is as if extended in time. In hockey sometimes you yourself are surprised by a combination which you, the dispatcher of the squad, thought up and executed by some intuitive signals you make not in moments but parts of moments, which is all the time you have at your disposal.

Improvisation does not mean lack of control. Within the squad there was a division of responsibilities, a kind of a division of work, each concentrating on what he did best. Why should Makarov force his way to the net if Krutov is the best to lead a single man attack on a lead pass? Why should Krutov control the puck for a long time if Makarov does this job brilliantly and is more often than anyone the first to cross the blue line and get the puck in the other zone? Why should I bother with all these things if my main task is to distribute passes? Why should Fetisov sit in the background if his joining in the attack causes panic among the ranks of the rivals, and Kasatonov or I can cover him?

In a few words, this was what we stressed in our play. And the basis was the usefullness of each one, the ability to substitute for anyone, and fulfil the other's responsibilities, maybe not as well, but not to blunder, not to disturb the general picture of the play.

Not everyone is equipped for it. The inclination towards improvisation depends not only on talent, partners, the team, but also on the makeup of your personality. Let my club slaughter all opposition, one after the other, let my line be considered one of the best, but if if I myself played with no unpredictability, without cleverness or improvisation, I was not emotionally satisfied. With the result, yes, but not with the way I had expressed myself on the ice, for that is what provides the beauty of our game, given to the spectators by us. These are not just words. I take this very seriously.

On every shift we strove to confuse. Two, three, five, ten faultlessly rehearsed combinations are fine, but would not produce the results of such confusion. To confuse, to stun, means to offer the

72

unexpected, the novel; to mask to the utmost the time and place of the decisive strike or strikes on the goal. And by quickly passing back and forth, by constantly moving in all different directions, by circling, we tried to make the heads of the defenders spin.

Of course, as in music, this leaning towards improvisation was based on knowing all the principles, on rehearsing and, of course, on the highest individual mastery by such exceptional masters. Was it possible to mix up Fetisov with Kasatonov, or Makarov with Krutov? Of course not. Everyone has his own style of skating.

And my first responsibility, as the dispatcher in charge of the organization and direction of a play, was to make good use of this maximal horsepower, to utilize this richness, this well of talent.

If, as people said soon after we began to play as a unit, that improvisation was our trade mark, then our language was the the pass. Playing the pass is my main game, but I had to pass to suit everyone. Makarov required a certain pass, Krutov another. And Fetisov? I knew that if he broke into the open, if he took the risk, he would finish the job – just as he knew he would get the puck, and that I would give it to him on time.

It is impossible to learn these things by heart, to cram them into your head as from a textbook. We did not practise detailed tactics beforehand, where for every player it would be strictly defined what, when, and how he had to carry out certain actions, and to which actions he did not have any rights. We did not go as far as scrupulously calculating our combinations. We spoke about that part of our game only rarely – a few words, perhaps, as we sat on the bench catching our breath in the heat of battle. But as soon as we left the ice palace, conversations about who should have gone out into the clear, who and when and to whom should have given a pass, became almost forbidden. We didn't discuss it because we did not feel it to be necessary.

Actually, even if we'd had the interest, we rarely had the opportunity. In the double rooms at Archangel or in the hotels in other cities we usually had other roommates. Makarov shared quarters with defenceman Sergei Starikov; Krutov and the well-known forward, Nikolai Drozdetsky, and I was with Volodia Zubkov. Fetisov and Kasatonov, inseparable friends then (but not now, even though they are teammates in New Jersey) always bunked together. Sometimes between themselves they discussed the game at an untimely hour. Now, I understand, they discuss nothing.

There was, I suppose, a single cause for a verbal debate: the failure of the team. With recognition as the premier squad on the club and on the National team came heavy responsibility, laid on ever so willingly by our coaches. When the team won they praised us, but invariably added that the other squads also contributed quite heavily. When the team, God forbid, lost, the fault was the Larionov Line's.

We lived with it the simplest way. We ignored it.

When things were going bad, though, and we did discuss it, the talk took an interesting course. Fetisov and Kasatonov were bearing grudges against Makarov, Larionov, and Krutov, who heated up and replied in kind. That is, the skirmish was between the defence and the forwards! In some things, borders change nothing.

Our ambition to be leaders and only that entered into our body and soul, and in all those years it never left.For a couple of years in the Soviet Union, the members of Dynamo offered us a serious threat, which they also brought to the select team the line of Vasily Pervukhin, Alexsander Bilillyatdinov, Sergei Svetlov, Anatoli Semenov and Sergei Yashin. I would not say that it happened often, but there were times when they won the inter-squad with us. In any case, they really made us run for it. All five of them were physically strong men, not lacking in height and speed. In Novogorsk, at the Olympic base near Moscow, we quite often battled with them, and not only on the ice. We also loved to measure our strengths playing minisoccer: hockey goalposts and five players per team.

Our line would beat the Dynamo Line sometimes by 14 goals! It would be 20-6 or 25-11. Such an embarrassment. If my team had managed to come out looking so bad, no matter in which game, I could not live with myself. I would lose my peace of mind and sleep. By the way, I would not call Fetisov and Kasatonov, nor Makarov and Krutov whizzes with a leather ball. I myself play a little better perhaps, but not that much, not enough to take all the credit myself. I am not Maradona. If one were to make a comparison between our members and those of the Senyonov line, perhaps we should have been winning anyway, but never with such a crushing score.

Therefore, we put a lot more desire, will and emotion into it, even on a green field during a half-serious training game without spectators. It was essential to keep our leadership, our reputation. But the Dynamo calmly dispersed after the game, which surprised me very much, defeat gone "like water off a duck's back." You can say what you want, but it is ambition, exactly that, which they lacked. They valued their colours casually. The same was true in hockey, and they have still not managed to become that power which our specialists foretold in their own time.

We also met face to face on the volleyball court. They were quite superior to us in height, and their forwards were each five to 10 centimetres taller than I am, but even here when the five of us pushed for it, and we almost always pushed, we had the best of them. Even in basketball we were better.

You see what it means when five young men value the reputation of their club? Ours was a world famous club consisting of five people. We respected it accordingly.

For almost a decade I lived in the centre of the world hockey stage. I have seen much and lived through a lot. And I have come to ask myself more often: what do you remember most?

It's still not the goals, the passes, and not even the victories, even though you turn yourself inside out for them. What remains is the enjoyment of the game. A game which is comparable to art. When the spirit of mutual creativity arises, it cannot be expressed in words! During such a time I cannot separate myself from Krutov, Makarov, Fetisov, and Kasatonov.

The Green squad was he, he, he, he, and I –and the other way around. Inseparable.

Chapter 6
OH, CANADA

I had visited the West many times, but until I joined the Vancouver Canucks my impressions were all superficial, fleeting, since hockey ate up so much of the time here. In addition there was the power of Tikhonov, such a combination of a dictatorship and of being in kindergarten, which did not allow us to show our faces anywhere. But this I knew from the first visit: when the Canadians from the NHL play as a unit for their country, the honor of the flag literally over-fills them. They never quit, never give up in battle, never give up hope.

The truth is that most Canadian NHLers aren't all that interested in the total Canada Cup competition. The idea of beginning an already over-long season weeks early to get ready to play West Germany or Finland or even Sweden or Czechoslovakia, does not excite them. Some of those selected decline. Prior to the 1988 Canada Cup even Wayne Gretzky said that he might not play, that another way had to be found to shorten the season or perhaps hold the series in a break during the NHL schedule. And, judging by the crowds for such matches in some cities, Canadian spectators share this lack of interest.

But Team Canada vs the Soviet Union – the best vs the best! Ah, then the flag is unfurled and the country stops to watch.

It goes back, of course, to the first Team Canada-Soviet Union series in 1972, the first time NHL players met the Soviet Nationals head-on. To this day some claim that was the greatest hockey series ever played: Eight games, of which Canadian fans heavily favored their team to win all eight, and easily. Instead, the team of Kharlamov and Alexander Yakushev and Vladislav Tretiak came to Montreal, gave up the first two goals, then came back to win 7-3. The Canadians came back to win the second game 4-1 in Toronto. The third, in Winnipeg, ended in a 4-4 draw, the fourth, in Vancouver, a 5-3 victory for our Nationals! This series that Canada was supposed to win easily now stood at 2-1-1 for the Soviet Union, with the next four games in Moscow!

If you consider it, the third-game tie made the series. An eight-game affair could have ended in a draw. The tie made it a best-of-seven and, barring another tie, assured an overall winner. North Americans understood best-of-seven. It is the way the Stanley Cup championship is settled.

They went to Moscow, to the Luzhniki Ice Palace – and our National team scored the last four goals in the third period for a 5-4 victory. One more win, and the NHL was beaten!

And then the flag unfurled. With one end of the Moscow Ice Palace filled with flag-waving Canadian fans, Team Canada won the sixth game 3-2, the seventh game 4-3 and the deciding game 6-5. In each case the winning goal was scored by Paul Henderson, with but two minutes and six seconds to play in Game 7 and 34 seconds remaining in Game 8!

Thus were sown the seeds of perhaps the greatest hockey rivalry of all. Eight games, settled in the final three minutes of the last game and only a one-goal difference in total, 32-31 for the Soviet Union! And there is an interesting footnote to the tale. As the Krutov-Larionov-Makarov forwards were united and immediately fit like magic, so did Team Canada assemble the line of Henderson and his Toronto Maple Leaf teammate, Ron Ellis, on the wings, and the hard-working, combative Bobby Clarke at centre. Of Canada's 32 goals, Henderson scored seven (tying team captain Phil Esposito and our Yakushev for the lead), Clarke three, and the tireless Ellis assisted on three. So well did they fit together that, upon the return to Canada, Maple Leafs team owner Harold Ballard said he would pay Philadelphia $1 million for Clarke's contract. Philadelphia was not interested.

I do not know how interest in future Canada Cup competitions will fare, or what form they will take. Perhaps, with the bars now down and Soviets playing in the NHL, the series will lose its lustre for the NHLers as it did once the best of Sweden, Czechoslovakia and Finland were seen on a regular basis in league play. But I know this: playing in that series was always a true challenge for our Nationals, and for our line.

I myself have played in three: in 1981, when our line was just formed and Team Canada beat us 7-3, then 8-1 in the final; in 1984, when Mike Bossy scored in overtime to beat us 3-2 in the semi-final and Canada went on to defeat Sweden in the first two matches of a three-game final, and in 1987, when some claim the three-game

Team Canada series rivaled and perhaps even surpassed the legendary meeting in 1972.

Four times we met. Our game in the round-robin series ended in a 3-3 tie, and each of the three games in the final finished 6-5 – the first two in overtime, the last decided with 86 seconds left in the third period. Our Nationals won the first, Team Canada the last two – again, the flag! – both on goals by Mario Lemieux, set up by Gretzky!

That series was an example of something we faced from our very first season. Our competitors, both in the Soviet Union and abroad, had one major aim: To neutralize the Larionov line. I do not mean to lessen the worth of the other lines, especially that of Bykov (Stelnov Starikov; Khomutov Bykov Kamensky) or the Semyonov line (Pervukhin Billilyatdinov; Svetlov Semyonov Yashin). But this is what came to be the rule: when the first line was attacking, the rest did so. We could feel their support. But as soon as we, for some reason, lowered the quality of our play, they also let up, or in any case failed to make the saves by coming up to take the lead in difficult moments.

To that effect, in that 1987 series, the three Canadian greats were put together for the first time – Gretzky and Lemieux on the wings with the massive Mark Messier at centre. They won the series, but I would not say they broke us. The 210-pound Messier did not spare either himself or his competitors. But he did not achieve anything worthwhile, he merely complicated my game. Under such conditions communication between the players of our line was broken. I did not direct the action of my teammates to the full extent, and could not establish a rhythm for the line. No, the lines played as equals – and as I understand it, this was viewed by our competitors as an achievement.

We had become used to such close attention. It spurred us on, made us look for new tactics, new tricks. It is amazing what things teams came up with in order to put out our fire! They tried two line changes when we were on the ice. They tried to lead us into their zone to limit our operating space. They had players shadowed, in particular the centre forward. And there was straightforward dirty playing, a petty or even a clear foul, in the hope of making Makarov or Krutov lose their balance. Both were known for their short tempers, and how they hurried to get back at an offender.

They came up with a lot of things to unbalance us. And I will not say that they were always unsuccessful. The Moscow Dynamo players, Anatoli Semyonov's line, managed to play on par with ours.

The same goes for the Czechoslovakian players, led by Dusan Pasek, and the Swedish line of Tomas Steen, Kent Nilsson and Hakkan Loob.All these centres were strong players, but I do not consider it showing off to say this: When everything was in order and we were in top form, it was hard to hold us back. Almost impossible. Few could manage it in those days.

We never resented this "special" treatment. In fact, it was somehow pleasant because they only carefully guarded and gave special attention to the strong players and squads. To have the same "compliment" paid by the stars of the NHL was like a pat on the back.

Not that they were always complimentary. I recall a time in Helsinki when compliments were the last thing on their minds...

My memories of that first meeting in the '81 Canada Cup are something of a blur. I was two months out of Voskresensk, a newcomer to the National team, and here I was, playing against men I'd heard and read about for years. It was a great feeling, and we won that last game so decisively, but so many other feelings were pressing in on me: the first trip to North America, the sights to see, the overwhelming *amounts* of things so difficult if not impossible to find at home... The time, the games, flew by.

But in April, 1982, at the world championships in Helsinki, it was a different story. It would be difficult to forget a single detail of our relationship with the Canadians in that one, particularly at the finish which, you might say, did little for international hockey relations.

Under the system in use at that time, we had beaten Canada 4-3 and 6-4 in the preliminary rounds. Now, in the final game, we played Czechoslovakia with the gold medal already ours. But the result was important to the Czechs and to Team Canada: If we won, Canada got the silver medal. If we lost or tied, Czechoslovakia got the silver and Canada the bronze.

We played to a 0-0 tie. The Canadians did not take it well. As we skated off the ice there they were: Bobby Clarke, Bill Barbour, Mike Bossy, Bryan Trottier – cursing us, making slicing motions with their hands across their throats and screaming:

"Just wait 'till December, you #$%$! You'll get yours!"

And we knew right away that the Super Series in Canada at the end of the year was going to be even more interesting than usual.

The question is asked: Did we "throw" that game to the Czechs! Did we give them the tie to keep the silver medal from the Canadians?

I don't know. If it was planned I was unaware of it. I tried to score. No one told us to go out and "throw" it. Maybe the veterans of the time were told, but as relative newcomers to the team, our line might not have been considered a necessary part of any scheme. And though it might come as a shock to North Americans, beating Canada is not the No. 1 priority of the Soviet National team. At least, not to the politicians who rule our game. To the players, yes, because we had the pride of wanting to test ourselves against the best. To Tikhonov, yes, because to him every game was the world championship final. But from the top of our hockey pyramid the word was "Losing to the Czechs or Swedes is not good – but don't you dare lose to the Americans!" Not the Canadians, the originators of our game. Politically speaking, Canada was a neutral country. America was not. Similarly, we could lose to the Poles – but we'd better not lose to West Germany!

So I doubt that the tie was "thrown" to the Czechs. We had the gold medal. The rest did not matter. But I know one game that was thrown. I know because I was told later, and because of what happened in the third period.

We were playing Dynamo Riga in the final game of the 1982 Soviet championships. Again, we already had the gold medal. But if Dynamo could get a win or a tie in that match, they would get the silver. And Mikhail Vasiliev, who had captained the National team in 1982 and had many friends among our own National team members, played for Dynamo.

And there we were, leading 2-0 with eight minutes left in the match. Krutov and I were buzzing around the Dynamo net, trying for the third goal. At our end, I threw myself in front of a puck that seemed destined for the net. All together, a satisfying shift for our line.

Some of our players did not think so.

"What are you doing that for?" they asked as we reached the bench. "They need two goals!"

Dynamo got their two goals, and second place. The game ended in a 2-2 tie. As they say in North America, "What are friends for?"

Team Canada had promised us a warm reception in the Super Series, and they kept their word. It began in Edmonton, where Gretzky scored a great goal and we lost 4-3. **SWEET REVENGE!** screamed one newspaper headline the next morning. But this was a six-game series, not a one-game affair, and we had used Vladimir Myshkin in goal, not Tretiak. In the next two games we played our netminding ace and shut out Quebec 3-0 and Montreal 5-0. Then it was Myshkin's turn again, and we lost 3-2 in Calgary.

For Tikhonov, that was enough. Our line was playing well despite missing Makarov, who was injured and could not make the trip and was replaced by Viktor Tuminev. But the series was tied at 2-2 and the coach was furious. Before the next game against Minnesota he held a long, tough meeting, yelled at us – and put Tretiak back in the net for the last two games. We beat Minnesota 6-3, and finished by defeating the Flyers 5-1 in Philadelphia.

In that match I was chosen the most valuable player for our team and Clarke for the Flyers. I considered it a great honor to share the award with him. I still remembered him from watching that first '72 series. He had long, curly blonde hair then and looked like an angel with no teeth, but he was a great player and leader, even if he did put Kharlamov out of the series with a chop across the ankle.

It seems he did not share my sentiments. As it was translated later to us, he said that it was an honor to win the award, and we had won the series, but we had also sent troops into Afghanistan! This saddened me. What did we have to do with that? We were hockey players in honest competition. What place did politics have on the ice with us?

Gretzky has said more than once that the next Team Canada-Soviet series should be played in Moscow; that it is only fair that the Soviets have the advantage of home ice and home country, and Team Canada the disadvantages of long travel, different food and accommodations and culture. I don't know how much difference it would make in the results, but it would be a worthwhile experience for the players and the fans who made the trip with them. At least it would destroy some misconceptions.

Take the matter of how Soviet players eat. Each time the National team toured, North American media would marvel at the way the National team could consume food! Columnists would write about it, going so far as to talk to hotel chefs to get actual figures on the amount served. They were correct – it was a large amount. But not for the reasons they thought.

It was not that we hadn't seen food of this kind. We simply hadn't seen so *much* of it, and such variety in seeming defiance of the seasons. I'm not speaking of lobster or frogs legs, but of basics. In training camp at home they made sure we had good food and plenty of it. The meals were balanced. There was no reason to complain. But cucumbers and tomatoes, for instance, were unheard of in the Soviet Union until August. Here time did not matter. There were strawberries and watermelon.

Our players come from working class families in a land of low wages and lineups. Such food could not be put on the table at home. And a mother weary from standing in line to get what she could had no time to talk to children about the manner and amount of food to be eaten. It was enough to get home, clean the house, put the meal on the table and go to bed to get ready to begin another day.

So, when our teams came to this land of plenty, they reacted like vultures. They took it all, and whatever they could stuff into their bodies, they did. Viacheslav Koloskov, the leader of our delegation, was astounded once as he watched my teammates destroy a smorgasbord table on the day of a game: spaghetti, chicken, meat, glass after glass of milk, cake.

"You cannot do this before a game!" he said. "Why has Tikhonov not warned you?"

I do not know. For me it was never an issue. In my Voskresensk days I'd been fortunate enough to meet a doctor who had explained proper dietary procedures to me. I knew what to eat and when to eat it. I knew my body, and treated it well. But for others not that fortunate, a visit to North America was not merely a great hockey experience and a chance to buy things unavailable at home. It was one long picnic table, and they more than did it justice.

But always, the eyes were on the hockey series. And from a North American point of view, the '84 and '87 Canada Cups had to be considered on a par with the legendary first meeting of '72. Our own viewpoint, naturally, was somewhat different.

We were a team rebuilding in the autumn of '84. Vasiliev had left to coach Dynamo. Fetisov was lost to us with a broken ankle suffered in a European Cup match in Italy just before the Canada Cup. We somersaulted without him. On the one hand we tried as much as was within our power. We wanted to keep up the reputation of the squad during the absence of its leader, and we played rather well. We did not hear an accusing word. But something passed over us, almost imperceptibly. I am not superstitious, but it was as if a black cat had crossed our path.

Or perhaps it was that a big cat had left us. The catlike Tretiak, goaltender without equal, professional hockey man through and through, had retired. Heading into the Canada Cup series without him, we felt orphaned.

Even those of us who were used to compliments coming our way from every direction automatically began to look back at Tretiak with appreciation, and as an example as far as his attitude towards our cause. During a game with Tretiak in goal, even during the most difficult moments, we did not look back in fear because we knew that in extreme situations Tretiak would save us, he would not let us down.

The loss of our "keeper" was made worse by the fact that there was no need for it. Tretiak could have still come out, but in the end, as with all of us, our homeless existence with its endless matches in the season, sometimes necessary and sometimes totally unnecessary, wore him out.

Tretiak had asked, "Give me a chance to be with my family just a little bit." But Tikhonov did not make an exception for our pride, our superstar, who had not even once over 15 years of hockey broken with the routine.

I believe I felt Tretiak's absence more acutely than my teammates. The great goalie was not formally listed in the first line, but in essence, he was inseparable from us. So why was I especially suffering? I was the centre forward. I was responsible not only for the recurrent combinations, but in the case of the failure of the attack, I must skate back at full speed to clean up, secure the defence. The defencemen are the first to await myhelp. And when Tretiak left, Fetisov and Kasatonov and I began to worry more about the rear. We began to feel nervous at times, began to make the wrong decisions because we did not want to see the puck in our goal. We were taking risks a little less often, improvised a little less often, and without that the game ceased to be the joy it once had been for us. As the commander, as the dispatcher of the squad, I could feel the heaviness, as if something were pressing down on my shoulders.

And again we found ourselves in a final preliminary round game with the opportunity to decide our own fate.

Alan Eagleson, the tournament director, had decided that Canada should play us in the last preliminary game to stimulate interest. And it was true: games involving other teams were not bringing big crowds. But the draw presented a bigger problem: if we beat Canada, then the Canadians would finish fourth – and thus we would play them in one semi-final while Sweden and the U.S. met in the other. The dream of a Canada-Russia best-of-three final before a capacity crowd would be wiped out. If Team Canada beat us, then the chances were good we would clash in the final.

We agreed with Eagleson. We wanted to meet Canada in the final. But we beat them 5-3 in that last game – a game I missed due to a slight knee injury and most memorable as the one in which Messier used his stick on Vladimir Kovin and cut his face for 21 stitches.

Two nights later, Sweden defeated the U.S. 9-2 in their semifinal. The following night in Edmonton, we faced Team Canada again. It was a game that will be discussed for years because of one play:

With the score tied 2-2 in overtime, Kovin broke out with Alexander Skvortsov, with only defenceman Paul Coffey back. Kovin attempted to draw Coffey to him, then passed the puck across to Skvortsov. But Coffey read the play, went down almost to one knee as he backed up, somehow blocked the puck with the shaft of his stick, and moved almost in the same motion toward our end before throwing the puck into the corner.

John Tonelli, whose hard work in the corners earned him the tournament award as Canada's most valuable player, battled on the boards one last time to take control of the puck and feed it across the front of our net. Bossy had barged into the crease, knocking the stick from Myshkin's hand as he himself was flattened by our defenceman. He was climbing to his feet as the puck came from Tonelli, and with the instinct of the great shooter he was able to recover and flip it into the net.

That quickly, at 12:29 of overtime, we were out of the competition. All that was left for us was to sneak out of the hotel that night and join Team Canada in the disco, then climb aboard the plane the next morning for the long flight home. Canada went on to sweep the first two games from Sweden to capture the Cup, and everyone agreed it had been a magnificent Canada-Russia match.

How could they know that in three years there would be four games at least as good and possibly better?

For me, the 1987 Canada Cup series began with a joke on Tikhonov – a joke he never realized was played.

Although some games were played elsewhere in Canada, the main site for the tournament was Hamilton, Ont. In a gesture of friendship and hospitality, Gretzky invited Fetisov, Makarov, Dave Poulin of the Philadelphia Flyers and myself to meet his family in nearby Brantford where he was raised and his father, Walter, had built the backyard ice rink on which Wayne had learned much of his game. The plan was that Walter would drive in and take us there.

Tikhonov said no. Anywhere outside of Hamilton was off-limits. It was out of the question. But Walter Gretzky arrived anyway, and we hit upon a plan.

We took Walter up to Tikhonov's room, introduced him to the coach, and said that Walter would very much like *him* to come to dinner also.

Tikhonov made a show of hesitating. "Let me think about it," he said. In a few minutes, we were heading for the car.

We had a fine time, but when Wayne offered us wine or beer, Tikhonov spoke for us. "No," he said. "Only Pepsi-Cola. And ice cream!"

We had Pepsi-Cola and ice cream – except when we went down to the basement to view the Gretzkys' trophy room. There, while Tikhonov ate his ice cream and drank his pop and a lookout was posted at the stairs, his players had their beer. Where there is will, there is a way.

As to the games themselves, how could they have been any better?

In the round-robin game we led 3-1 in the second period, but Raymond Bourque scored on a power play before the period ended, and Gretzky earned Team Canada the tie with a goal from Messier and Glenn Anderson at 17:33 of the third. Now we were in Montreal to open the three-game final on the same ice where Gretzky had operated so effectively from behind the net, feeding pass after pass in those two one-sided victories in '81.

I remember walking out into the empty Forum 90 minutes before the first match, staring at that space behind the net and thinking about Gretzky. If our line was against his, how would I battle him? What would be the best tactic? Before the 8-1 loss in 1981 the coaches had held a long meeting, bringing out the blackboard and showing us what he did behind the net. But the ice was not a blackboard, and Gretzky not a piece of chalk.

The first result was promising, although not at the beginning. Team Canada scored three unanswered goals in the third period – the last by Gretzky – to overcome a 4-1 deficit and take a 5-4 lead. The day before, he and Tretiak had made international hockey history by teaming to do a television commercial – for an underarm deodorant. Obviously, friendship had ceased. This time, though, we had the answer. Khomutov scored 32 seconds later and Alexander Semak, known for his powerful shot, got the winner on a slapshot at 5:33 of overtime.

I remember the second game for two things: One, in the second overtime period, I fed a pass to Krutov, who already had two goals. He snapped the shot – and Grant Fuhr, the goaltender, snapped out his glove to stop it. A fraction less quickness of the hand, and the series would have been ours!

Unfortunately, it was also the game in which Team Canada coach Mike Keenan decided to put Gretzky and Lemieux on the same line. He had resisted the temptation, calling such a move ''counter-productive'', but they were so effective on power plays and in four-on-four situations that he finally yielded.

That game Lemieux scored a hat-trick, including the winner at 10:07 of the second overtime. Gretzky assisted on all three, and on two other goals. Two nights later, after we'd led them 3-0 and 4-2 in the first period, it was Lemieux on a drop pass from Gretzky with 1:26, beating Sergei Mylnikov for the winning goal and the Canada Cup.

We'd had our chances. Ours was not a team used to losing after a three-goal lead. But always we seemed to tire. It has always been a riddle for me: Players are chosen for our Canada Cup team June 25. From July 15 to Sept. 1 we do nothing but train for that one tournament. The Canadians don't begin picking their team until Aug. 5. By the time of the big games, we are washed out and they are still fresh. But we keep doing it that way. Are our hockey officials too proud to learn? Too stubborn to change?

The winning goal in the last game was Lemieux's 11th of the tournament. Of the 11, Gretzky had assisted on nine. What a pity for us that Keenan wasn't stubborn enough to keep them apart!

That Canada Cup loss was more than another defeat at the hands of Team Canada. For our line, it was the beginning of the end. For us, the best of times – a string of continuous successes – were the four seasons from 1981 through 1984. The time flew by as one happy moment. Continuous victories, continuous happiness from the game. It seemed that this is how it would be forever.

I remember my first years in the CSRA. We were all young and obsessed solely by hockey. Hockey and hockey and nothing else. Only Makarov was married then, and there was nothing to inter-fere, to hinder the rest of us from playing. All the fragments of hockey life were somehow in full view. I was always respectful towards our rivals. I did not put on airs even during the time when my head could have been spinning with all the success. But then, in those years, the thought never even entered my head that some-one could be superior to our line in anything.

And then the pieces began to fall off our hockey machine.

In 1984, it was as though we were cursed. It wasn't just the loss of Fetisov and the retirement of Tretiak. Other troubles surfaced.

They began when we lost Yuri Moiseev. The departure of the assistant coach meant a drastic change in the conditions to which we'd become accustomed. He had been our go-between with Tikhonov, a builder of bridges between the two shores. He could do this like no other. And now the bridge was washed away.

Until the fall of 1984 there were, as they say, no questions and no problems. We played together for the sake of our own joy, for the sake of the team and for the spectators' pleasure. We also relaxed together. Everything was okay with us. We lived as a mini-team, which did not in the least appear in opposition to the team as a whole. A mini-team must be a well-knit unit. And that is what our line was.

Moiseev was capable of taking on the initiative. He could bring something of his own into the life of the team; conduct training in a novel way; relate to everyday problems in a nonstandard way. He even let some violations of discipline slide, as if turning a blind eye. He punished, but in his own way: Everything that was going on remained within the collective. No dirt was taken outside. But, at the same time, the guilty people knew that for this humane treatment they would have to work without sparing themselves.

But, one by one, the obstacles began to appear on what had been the smooth ice surface of our hockey lives.

Sometimes the stumbling blocks were purely psychological.

We needed Olympic gold at Sarajevo. The Soviet select team needed to retrieve the status of champions at any cost, which had been lost at Lake Placid four years earlier. For Tikhonov, a second miss of such a calibre would mean a crashing end to his career. No one would ever forgive him. But not even that really mattered. We, the players, craved this victory, this Olympic victory, which is valued above anything else in our country. And precisely this super responsibility paralyzed us. The fear of making a mistake, even the smallest, led to careful checking every second. Genuine improvisation was the last thing on our minds. We won the gold, and our line performed well, but it would be exaggerating to give it an A+. No one knew that better than my partners and I.

Or consider the 1987 World tournament in Vienna. Two factors immediately proved to be fatal to our game.

The major test of the season took place in April, at the end of our season. We arrived spent after 10 months of constant touring and, mostly, 10 months of meetings, more than half of them held for no apparent reason. Because of our extremely rare appearance at home with our families – a burden felt more and more with the years, to the point where it was unbearable – we were emotionally exhausted.

The coaches, to phrase it politely, did not do anything to raise our spirits. They, for example, had organized a walk in the park, and whether or not you wanted to go, you had to go and breathe the fresh air "hand-in-hand" with the other players. But, perhaps I wanted to spend some time curled up on a sofa with a book? No!

I really envied the Swedes. They came to Vienna with their wives. We could not even dream about that! And what happened? All the while Tikhonov was saying that the Swedes "are not a hockey team, you can write them off already." But the Swedes had seriously prepared themselves for the championship, got themselves together in the decisive moment, and became the champions.

Another character trait of our squad came through in Vienna. On the eve of the meeting with the Canadians, Tikhonov suddenly and very firmly forbade Fetisov and Kastatonov from attacking, "or else I'll strip you of your officer's stripes!." But our game depended on precisely that active participation of every player in every play. That was why we were beginning to lose a lot from the very start: because we could not count on the support of the defencemen on an attack. The final score was 0-0, against a very modest Canadian team that consisted of average players. For some strange reason Tikhonov thought that we should fear the Canadian counter-attacks. And the Canadians, in my opinion, were not even thinking about that.

Judging by everything that happened, the fateful swan song of our squad was to be at the 1988 Olympic Games in Calgary. We hadn't discussed it much during the winter, but we all understood without saying that you cannot stop the course of time, and that it was very unlikely that the same lineup will be defending the reputation of Soviet hockey. Fetisov and Makarov were getting close to 30; there was more and more talk about invitations from NHL clubs, which would undoubtedly do us and our hockey a lot of good. I did not hide my intentions to stop playing under the CSRA banner, and to transfer to Khimik, or to join the Canucks. Or, the coaches could have divided us among different lines to help the young players.

Well, if it was to be our last song, we would sing it well! We concentrated on preparation, determined not to wind up with mud on our faces. This served as a good irritant for each of us and all of us together. And when the moment came we played lightly, beautifully, as if on wings. I would give us an A+. In Calgary we were lucky enough to combine the result and the beauty of the game itself, as we had always strived to do. And in the end, we brought home the gold.

Then came the 1989 World championships in Sweden – and already, strictly speaking, we were not quite the same line.

Kasatonov was in the lineup, but playing with different partners. The first crack in the unit! We four had lost personal contact and mutual understanding with him. We could not see eye-to-eye on the principle questions and did not wish to play together. Instead of Kasatonov they gave us Viktor Shiryaev, from Kiev. He was quite a decent defenceman, who tried not to ruin the game. Meanwhile Alexei, with his new partners, felt lost, and his game reduced to average.

And what about us? We were sticking together and trying to do all we could to maintain the high reputation of each other, and the four of us together. It was not going to be easy.

The playing of our line was considered to be an example for almost a decade. From the outside we seemed to many an irreproachably perfectly tuned mechanism. But we were humans, not robots. I do not like the comparison to a machine, an automaton, or a computer. We invested a tremendous amount of human emotion and inspiration into the game; each of us was capable of that. However, if there is an insistence to compare us to modern technology, then the mechanism of our playing was rather complicated and fickle, and to maintain it in perfect running order was very difficult. There were no guarantees except for the ones that we ourselves could give. As soon as there was a weak spot somewhere, every one of us would feel it, trying to patch up the gap in the ship.

Life, however, had decided otherwise.

The last season of our squad was plastered all over the press and television: The confessions and scandals of Larionov and Fetisov.

I had published my open letter to Tikhonov. Fetisov was supposed to play in the NHL in New Jersey in the season following the Olympic Games, and we assumed that we would go to the NHL in a year after him. But bureaucrats of every suit and color and department harassed Viacheslav and continued to harass him until he finally left without getting anywhere for all his pains. He lost the entire season – and we lost the best defenceman in the world. As if all this were not enough, the season turned out to be the most complicated, dramatic and unsuccessful we'd ever endured.

The day before leaving for the world championships, I told a journalist, "Everything will be okay. We are still trying to find our

Igor

Soviet National Team at Lenin's Tomb, Red Square, Moscow.

K-L-M Line at Central Army Complex, Moscow.

Igor and game shots at Luzinlch Ice Palace, Moscow.

Fetisov, Kasatonov, Krutov, Igor and Makarov.

Makarov and Igor, summer training.

Krutov, Fetisov, Igor and Makarov getting set for practice.

Igor at practice.

Tikhonov talks to his players.

Igor vs. Czech., 1989 World Championships, Stockholm.

Fetisov, Igor and Helmut Balderis at Archangel.

Pat Quinn and Igor fishing in Vancouver.

Elena and Igor doing the dishes.

Alyonka and Elena.

Alyonka and Igor.

Alyonka and Igor at bedtime.

play, we are re-establishing old ties. What we need, what we really need, is for luck to go our way in Sweden."

Every type of sport has its own jargon. "Fluke" or luck is what hockey players and soccer players hope, to win by a fluke or luck. Not the kind of luck that suddenly falls from the sky. No. But there are situations in hockey where, no matter how beautifully a squad played out a manoeuvre, a little bit of luck would not hurt. For example, for the puck to go right inside the corner of the net instead of hitting the post, for the pass to a teammate to land exactly on the curve of the stick.

We went to Stockholm, and tried to ignore the rumors swirling around us. Soviet hockey leaders, it was whispered, were suggesting that there was no special need to win here. If we lost, they could always get rid of the undesirable senior coach, Tikhonov! We regarded this talk as insubstantial, but it persisted for a long time.

We played, but in the beginning the play of our squad was not going well, try as we might. In our game, a lot depends on the inner makeup of a man, on his emotions at the time, and the situation had turned out to be more complicated than I expected.

The conflicts of the season, on the lips of literally everyone, including the western correspondents accredited in Moscow, were intensified for us due to injuries. I do not remember a more unsuccessful season as heavy injuries for myself go: the fracture of my ankle in November, and just as I was getting back to normal, my fractured rib (suffered Dec. 26 in Canada but not X-rayed and diagnosed until Jan. 12). Krutov had also missed many a game after a back injury Jan. 4 in Pittsburgh. Fetisov had to train by himself for two months after refusing to apologize for a newspaper article in which he was sharply critical of the senior coach and said he didn't want to play for his team anymore. Only Makarov played the year without interruption, and he looked good from the very first match.

Communication was not as it used to be during a game. As the commander I could feel it, and I was very troubled because I was responsible for the interaction between players. Our mutual understanding was faltering somewhat. It is not by accident that I talked so much about improvisation. You cannot get it by calculation. It only happens during the lucky days of the player. Throughout the whole Swedish championship we were suffering. We wanted it, we were burning, and it was not turning out for us.

Fortunately, the second squad was saving the day, the line of Andrei Khomutov, Viacheslav Bykov and Valeri Kamensky. But the rumors about our alleged evil intentions and insidious cunning had spread more and more, and we were aware of them. We wanted to sing our swan song. We sort of knew the notes, but the melody was not coming out. But during the most important match, with the Canadians, we sang away, for we needed this victory like no one else.

We had no luck in Sweden. This is a fact.

I am the dispatcher, and I could feel it under my skin. Despite Fetisov's forced inactivity, and Krutov's and my own injuries, we were adequately prepared. Quite tolerably so. We were prepared to solve any problem, as usual, within our squad. And even more so, since Viktor Shiryaev had fit into the game nicely. I did not even feel the absence of Kasatonov.

So, why did luck turn away from us, match after match?

We had spent a lot of emotional strength, especially Fetisov and I, towards the struggle with Tikhonov's rules. We needed maximal concentration, but something was whirling and spinning in our consciousness. The recent worries had been far too serious.

We could not have known that the whole history of our confrontations with Tikhonov was near its completion, almost finished. This, perhaps, was the root of the problem. Finding yourself on the same team with a coach you hate fiercely, it is very difficult to show good hockey. It is simply impossible. Because you need to play for someone, not only yourself and not only for spectators, but for someone else yet, someone who will support you, and advise you.

We clearly lacked the emotional reserves, when at every step of the way, we heard the coach's innuendos, transparent innuendos that went something like:

"You see, I have told you that they are totally unprepared for the championship, that they are falling apart. I took them on. I would win even without them."

Up until the deciding match with the Canadians, Tikhonov would repeat this at every opportunity, just changing the words a little, as though his aim in life became to instill this thought in everyone around him. When Bykov's squad played very well in the tournament, which is unquestionable, but lost its mini-match 3-0 with the Canadian line against it, and we won ours 4-0 as we took the championship, 5-3, then it seemed that Tikhonov's game was up. But he has such an ability to name white as black. The broken record played on:

"Everything would have been normal. It's just that the guys from Bykov's squad were a little tired. And I would have won the championship anyway, even without Larionov's line."

Let that be on Viktor Vasilevich Tikhonov's conscience. There are many other things, also, a lot more significant.

I do not understand how Tikhonov could juggle reality so much. After the championship, Fetisov and Makarov, two members from our squad, joined the symbolic select team of the world. How can that be any insignificant detail?

I have always been indifferent to the fact whether I score or not, and what my personal sports credentials were. The main thing was that the playing of the squad was working. However, it is pleasant to remember that in the same game with the Canadians I scored twice. One goal came after Fetisov's flick from the blue line, and the other one turned out to be even more beautiful. Krutov and I came out two-on-two against the Canadian defenceman, Dave Ellett of the Winnipeg Jets. I noticed that Krutov was somewhere far off, slowed down a little and then decided to finish the attack on my own. Canadian defencemen, as a rule, do not get tricked, you cannot fool them with trick moves. But it turned out differently here. I pretended to move towards the centre as if waiting for Krutov. I let go of the puck a little bit, and saw from the corner of my eye that Ellett transferred his weight onto his outside leg. I cut suddenly to the other side, made a sharp turn, and from a 45-degree angle threw the puck between the goalie's shinpads.

Thus it was not Calgary, where we once more found our wings, but Sweden at the World championships, where they witnessed the swan song of our line. It was a hard song to sing, but we managed the final chord anyway. Despite everything, we departed with dignity: In the final, we played as in our old best times.

Now the waiting began. It was not a happy time. The decision to transfer to Khimik has already been made. I would go back to the city of my hockey youth, or I would join the Vancouver Canucks. One was as good as the other. But please, let the decision be made!

I waited with an aching nostalgia for a time that could not be returned, for the fantastic time when the Larionov Line performed on the ice of many cities and countries. Without this very same line, it would be difficult for me to live on. Very difficult.

The best years of my sports fate apparently were behind me. It was not a matter of age. I felt that I still had three or four years to play at a respectable level. But a hockey player is dependant upon the group in which he plays. Very rarely is he lucky with his teammates. And no one had been luckier than I.

Chapter 7
NIGHTMARE!

All hockey players, all of us, have our own caprices. We are engaged in a type of work in which it is impossible to paint a picture or plan ahead of time. We can only wait for the unexpected from around the corner, surprises that have a minus side or, more rarely, a plus. This is the nature of the game. It is unpredictable. For that reason it is attractive to millions of people.

We, creators of the hockey spectacle, are dependent on chance, on its grandeur and its fickleness. With this uncertainty, naturally, comes superstition: someone has put his skates on left foot first; that is why we have lost the game today. There are others even sillier.

Am I superstitious?

Perhaps not. Today I no longer experience trembling in the knees before fortune. There were some things. If I sleep during the day, on the day of the match, that means I will play well, and then it will not be embarrassing to look into the eyes of people, friends and acquaintances. But, if I do not doze off for at least half an hour, that is a disaster.

Sleep is a total science on its own. A long time ago I read about it in the magazine SCIENCE AND LIFE. I know myself that during the day one can dream up the devil knows what. Even if I was not anxious or nervous, if there had been no trouble, if everything seemed okay. But you can have nightmares so real that you awake and do not believe that it didn't really happen. When you come to your senses from this sticky and heavy dream and see everything is in order and understand that life continues, you receive a moment of childhood bliss.

Once my fate took such a sharp turn that even today, with more than three years already passed, I believe and yet I do not quite believe that it is all behind me. Such is the heavy sleep at noon. Such a nightmare, such a plain absurdity that could not be otherwise than in a stupid dream.

But this nightmare, this absurdity, alas, did not appear in a dream. It was reality. And the uncanny hallucination lasted neither an afternoon nor a day, but months. More than half a year.

Life was moving along its course. In hockey I was in everyone's sight. I was as if swimming on the waves on a cruiser yacht, easily cutting through the waves with such speed that the ocean breeze was pleasantly blowing on me. The wind was filling the sails.

This was the fifth year of my playing on the first squad, with Fetisov, Makarov, Krutov and Kasatonov. Playing was such a pleasure to us and to the spectators. It was also beneficial for our team and the club and the National selects. A misfire only happened once – in April, 1985, at the Prague Golden Tournament, which did not turn out to be gold for us, but bronze. After four seasons, after one complete Olympic cycle when we didn't know of any serious troubles on the rink, the Prague tournament was as a tub of icy water poured on us.

Soon after our return from Prague, we got together in the popular restaurant "Soviet", where the flourishing merchants would gather in their time. We did not come to eat. We talked among ourselves, as men, very seriously. No one specifically blamed our squad, us, for the collapse at Prague. But we were used to taking the troubles of our club on our shoulders. That is why we took such a result harder than the rest.

Then we dispersed for holidays. In different directions. Makarov and I went down to the Black Sea, to Guduat, to unwind and to rest up. And further on, in the course of the year, our usual forced life began with its structured boring gatherings. We were back on our daily routine.

The tournament put on by the newspaper IZVESTIA approached. It was December, 1985. There was nothing foreboding, as they say, no misfortune in sight. The tournament went on, after which there was a planned tour by the CSRA, a superseries in North America. Six matches with clubs from the NHL. A large part of the CSRA team was preparing for the tour as members of the National team. The departure for New York was planned immediately after the tournament. Everything went according to plan, as usual.

On the day before the last game with the National team of Czechoslovakia, on the morning of December 21st, just before the warmup, Vladimir Filippovich Vasilev, senior coach for Khimik, approached me. In those days he was preparing a youth National team for the World Championship in Canada. This team was also stationed at the Novogorsk base, only in a different building. He came to the hall, where there is a coaches' "box," and called me over to the side.

"Listen, Igor, I don't know exactly, but I've heard some trouble has come up concerning your departure, some formalities with your passport."

I mechanically rolled here and there along the boards, stretching my legs, I heard the words, but they did not sink in immediately.

"What delay? What the hell kind of formalities? I've been abroad a hundred times."

"I don't know, Igor. There is a delay with the passport, with the issuing of the passport."

Feeling fenced in, I asked: "What can it be? What does it mean?"

"Believe me, I don't know what it is. The situation is that you cannot leave. I simply wanted to warn you, so you could be prepared for it."

"Okay, okay, thank you, Vladimir Filippovich."

It was like a lightning bolt out of the blue.

During the pregame warm up I was as if drugged. What happened?

Why suddenly had these formal complications come up now?

How was one to understand it?

Why did this outsider, someone who has no ties with the CSRA, tell me about it?

What was I to do now?

I was at a loss. I was hoping that it was some kind of misunderstanding. Maybe the information was not completely correct, although Vasilev was not one for hearsay and gossip.

I went out to play against the Czechs. No one, not Tikhonov nor anyone else, would say anything to me. We finished the match, with the Czechs winning 3-1. No one gave me even half of an idea why this mess was emerging now. I was not lacking optimism, all the same, and chased out unpleasant thoughts.

The next day the training session was to be at five in the afternoon, and then we were to immediately leave for the country base at Archangel, spend the night there and go directly to the airport. The team was outfitted. (For tours, they always dressed us a little better: a nice and new coat, hat, suit, and shoes, all modern, imported and labelled – all of this so that the delegation is set off abroad and would not be ashamed to be seen in public.)

In accordance with how things are done at home, I said goodbye to my parents, saying not a word about my own troubles. We sat down for a minute before the long journey I was about to take, as is customary with Russians.

Thanks to Vasilev, I was no longer calm. That is why I drove to the training session in my own car. Usually all the guys leave their cars at home or in the garage before going abroad. Those who have them, that is.

Doubts were already gnawing at me, but I was still hoping for something. "Miracles" happen in our country. Perhaps this was just some bureaucratic nonsense, a mix-up in the red tape, and nothing more.

I finished training, took a shower, ate an orange and left the locker room.

That was when they called me into the coaches' room and "explained".

"Thus and thus, there is a delay with your passport. The situation is unforeseeable. But don't you worry about it, don't lose spirit. Understand, something is being planned across the ocean, some kind of conspiracy, as if some action is being prepared to somehow keep you abroad. For now, stay calm. Now your main goal is the championship of the world in Moscow. Everything depends on you, on your condition, on your shape, on how you will in these next few months prove yourself. Depend, accordingly, on further developments of events."

That was all that was said.

It made no sense. Why should I suddenly have to prove myself? To whom? What did this imply? A code message warning that it was not desirable for such a person as Larionov to travel abroad?

But what was there left to do? I said goodbye to the guys, and drove home.

I dreamed up some story for my parents. I did not want to upset them. I was at a loss. What is there left to make a hockey player happy, when he is actually on the airplane ramp and they turn him away; when he waits and waits and prepares and prepares for the games in Canada, and they deprive him of all of this for no reason?

But the blues still did not set in. There was still a glimmer of hope that all this was temporary, that soon all would fall into place, that I would return again and become a full member of the CSRA and the National team.

After about two days they phoned me at home and said that allegedly a decision was being made, and that apparently I would be able to depart in the next few days for Canada. Then all of this was stopped. Again no one explained it plainly.

Did I believe there was a threatening provocation around me? Nonsense! Doubts about this did not arise. Not because I was a superpatriot from a colorful poster. No. Even then I knew myself well enough, I was sure of myself, in all my life's principles. Neither before that nor after, did even a hint of a plan come to me to change the Soviet Union for the United States, for example. If I had wanted this, I could have done it at several opportunities.

But in January, 1986 all there was left for me to do was to watch on television those matches which I had dreamed of being a part. The broadcasts were recorded, but I was given the opportunity to watch them directly at the telecentre in Ostankino. Three, four or five o'clock in the morning I'd make the drive to the studio to watch those matches in which I should have been playing.

I learned later that at press conferences in different cities in the U.S.A. and Canada, it was often asked, "Why isn't Larionov in the line-up?" The answers given? Stories about my fragile health, about the illness that has suddenly befallen me. Larionov was suffering from tonsillitis, he had a chronic condition of this, that or the other.

All I could do was wait. The thick fog which blocked the road to the West for me would not disperse itself. I told myself, and my friends told me, that okay, I would miss this tour, that for some reason they didn't want me to go to Canada – but further on down the road everything would be in order.

Let us imagine the improbable: In the birthplace of hockey (Canada) they were after me. But not in every country were they waiting as to ensnare Larionov in a net. I had missed the Canada tour, but surely that would end the problem.

In February the CSRA planned a trip to Italy for the European Cup championship. When the CSRA team returned, the National team would immediately go to Sweden for three friendly matches.

And so, after the Soviet Union championship matches, they again drove us to Archangel. Again, I heard the words:

"Everything is normal. You're going."

They shook hands with me. They wished me well.

The trip to the airport was scheduled early in the morning. We whiled away the evening at the base. Some played cards or billiards and some were engrossed in television. Others stood in line at that single telephone.

And the team, almost the whole team, already knew that I was not going. And no one told me about it. I only found out about it later. This made an impression on my memory like a scar.

It was not all so simple. My teammates knew, but I suppose

that they did not want to upset me. Possibly they, as I, had hoped that all of this was a misunderstanding. I wanted badly to believe this.

When we were taking the bus to the base on the eve of our departure, Tretiak said to me, "Don't worry, you're going. Your passport has been signed." He was Lieutenant-Colonel Tretiak now, a responsible worker for the CSRA, not the goalkeeper who'd been as a wall in our net. He was with us as head of the CSRA delegation. I believed him. I felt a weight off my heart. The word of Tretiak was trustworthy. I was going. I went to bed particularly early.

"Rise and shine!"

This was our floor monitor, one of us hockey players who went through our small rooms bringing us to reality from the world of dreams. I jumped out of bed, washed, brushed my teeth, shaved, and put on my tie.

At 4:30 thirty in the morning the assistant coach, Boris Mikhailov, paid me a visit.

"Igor, understand, the situation is such that you are not going."

I could not contain myself.

"Again I'm not going! *Again,* do they want catch me in a trap, or what? Now the Swedes want me too?"

"What can I do about it?" he asked. "They did not want to upset you last night."

Con artist! And at 4.30 in the morning it's okay to upset someone? I was not a child, to be treated in such a way. And why suddenly this touching concern, as real as soap bubbles? I would not take to hard drinking over this news!. Say it simply – *humanely!* Simply explain why I cannot go! Tell me what was *happening!*

Mikhailov mumbled under his breath like a schoolboy trying to recite a poem from memory:

"Again, formalities, a delay with your passport..."

"I've *heard* all this. It does not cure me any more. I'm *tired* of it."

"Igor, go to the political division of the CSRA at 10 tomorrow, and they will explain everything."

All I wanted to do was put an end to this senseless conversation.

"Okay, good," I said. "I'll go."

The whole team boarded the bus, and I returned to Moscow. Once again I had prudently brought my Zhiguli. In half an hour I was at home and making up another story for my parents.

I did not go to the political division the next day. What was I to find here? Was I to listen again to the same old awkward set

100

of empty phrases, spun around and around in circles? They did not want to speak the truth, or did not know it. Either way, it would not make it any easier for me.

This second hit was below the belt, but I took it easier than the first time. It was not such a shock, such a flabbergasting event. On the other hand, my patience was exhausted.

There was not a truth to be reached from anyone, and this was the hardest, most agonizing thing about it. I tried somehow to distract myself. I saw friends more often, depending on their support in this difficult moment in my life.

I am not a reserved person, I love people, value real human interaction. In this burdensome, wholly unclear and suspicious circumstance, which was obviously drawn out, which was all the more like a blind alley, any sincerity, or compassion was appreciated.

"When misfortune comes, open the gates," so goes the saying.

All life is broadly and richly reflected, it seems, in Russian proverbs. It is not for nothing that Ronald Reagan liked our proverbs. He used them very successfully in his speeches during Gorbachev's visit to the United States, and also during his own visit to Moscow.

In the middle of a clear day I hit the crossroads of some sort of "enemy" powers, and in the end fell out of the sphere of hockey, where I had spent many a year. What the hell kind of a hockey player was I – on the National team, yet not taking part in International meetings?

Degradation. Loss of professional skill. Call it what you like. And there was a cost outside of hockey. I suddenly felt an emptiness around me, a vacuum. At home the phone which earlier rang off the wall, which I had to unplug when I wanted some peace, was quiet. Acquaintances who'd previously tried to catch my attention – just "happening" to cross my path to nod in a friendly way or shake hands and ask "How are things going, old man?", or ask for one of the club's hockey sticks – these people suddenly vanished. Did they evaporate, or what? That cloud that used to fly around me, to buzz around me importunately, blew quickly in an unknown direction.

I should have been happy to breathe easier, but, I must admit, it grated upon me. Many turned away from me, having heard about my troubles. Certainly there was more than enough hearsay and gossip. I could almost hear them:

"Have you heard, Igor has been denied travel privileges!"

"What are you saying, how can it be?"

"What has he gotten up to now, do you know by any chance?"

101

"Yes, yes, people who know from trustworthy sources have told me. You see, it has to do with..."

There was not a shortage of fabrication: black market dealings, money intrigues, etcetera. Hearsay for many in the country is pleasure. They don't need any bread as long as they can relish in someone else's personal life. And here they had found receptive soil. The hero himself, that is I, knew nothing. In the press there was not even a hint that something strange was going on with me.

I thought over a lot of things about life.

People around me were divided into two camps. The majority had forgotten both my home phone number and those corridors in the sports arenas where they could run into me. I became a disgraced hockey player. I did not regret this for a long time. I looked at it in a sensible way. For the most part these people were from the category of spongers, those who have to surround themselves with stars and be on familiar terms with them, and to boast about it before others. No loss there.

But then, friends remained. But not all of them. Not all conducted themselves in the same way. This was also a good lesson for me. It was as if I had seen them on a well-developed, quality negative piece of film.

My childhood friends from Voskresensk became still closer to my heart. Some of my Muscovite friends showed warmth, sincerity which I in general did not expect of them. Fetisov, Krutov and Makarov behaved normally towards me. It would have been different, if these events were happening not in the first year of perestroika. Later, I would guess, they would have behaved more actively, decisively in my support. The irony is that a year or two later, this useless detective story could hardly have happened.

It was not a total vacuum. The ranks of the people that I met with or talked with noticeably thinned out, but in this was its own plus side: it had been a good object lesson for me. I did not at all feel lonely and deserted by everyone. I had been very, very lucky that at this time I had already come to know Lena Batanova.

We met accidentally. I liked her immediately. But, I admit, such a thing had happened before in my life.

She knew nothing about hockey and could not have cared less. But as a figure skating champion she, too, had felt the unjust sting of false accusation. She and her partner had switched coaches in justifiable circumstances, and missed an Olympic Games trip they were scheduled to make as the third Soviet pair. With Lena I did not have to explain. She understood.

With every day, with each new meeting, when I tried to tear myself away from the training camp to see her by telling all the truths and lies, Lena brought forth all the more warmth to my heart. I could not have fathomed this as a growing feeling, this necessity to see and listen, and listen and see her more.

Apparently, I love proverbs no less than Reagan does: "There is no bad without good."

When grief piles up on you, they say these words, attempting to calm you. You do not take in these words in the beginning or only just a little bit. What kind of good is there, when everything falls apart like a house of cards? But human wisdom fits into all of life's situations.

Now then, being this hockey hermit, under this form of "house arrest", I could see Lena to my heart's content without any problems, without having to lower myself, without having to use the almost never satisfactory excuses to the coach to let me go off the base as my heart wanted to. If nothing else, I now had plenty of time for this.

We had known each other for almost a year, but I had gotten into a complicated mess and her attitude meant a lot to me.

Lena suffered with me, quietly, like a woman, without any sort of loud words or council about the smallest thing. But one cannot deceive a heart. More than ever in these times, I reacted very sensitively towards everything and everyone. I felt that she took my pain as her own, as if she wanted to take it upon herself.

I was no longer a beardless youth. I was 25 years old. I was independent materially and by Soviet standards very well off. Thoughts about a family and children had already come to me. And now there was Lena.

Towards the middle of February a very funny picture was being drawn on the map of the world: the popularity of Larionov did not grow by days, but by hours. More and more countries appeared, using all the truths and lies, craving to receive him as a new citizen. I still did not get to go to Canada, or Italy. But Sweden was next. And my superiors left me no doubts that my exile was over.

It was curious how those conversations with me about my situation were conducted confidently, in tones that excluded any sort of doubt concerning the trustworthiness of what had just been said.

"You did not go to Italy, but don't hang your head," I was told. "Train with the National team and get ready. Very soon, there will be a trip to Sweden. You are going to Sweden, do you understand?"

Oh, I understood, all right. To believe it was another matter.

Again, I drove my Zhiguli along the sad, traditional route to the National team camp at Archangel. There were only two other vehicles there – the team's Ikarus bus and a personnel carrier Volga with a soldier at the wheel. Tikhonov's car.

I am not a child, I understand that if they had twice given me the brush-off, then they could do it a third time. They could again talk the old nonsense without explaining anything to me, and then disperse. Could, and would.

I was training with the members of the CSRA who had not made the National team. Work went on, full-fledged work. The National team was to return from Italy in the evening. The next day was the trip to Sweden.

A friend called me in the morning.

"Igor, today in PRAVDA they published a list of the team, those who are going on the tour. Your name is not on it."

I asked him again:

"Are you sure?"

"Yes, I reread it twice. I phoned to warn you."

I approached Vladimir Yurzinov, faithful assistant of Tikhonov. It was about 5 p.m., and the team had not yet flown in.

"Vladimir Vladimirovich, with the situation here, maybe it is worth it for me to leave."

Yurzinov as usual waved his hands about, trying to calm me down:

"There is nothing to worry about, Igorek."

"The list of the touring team was published in PRAVDA, and I'm not on it. It is clear that I am not going. You know that PRAVDA would not lie."

"No, no, everything is normal. Now, we will wait for Viktor Vasilevich. They are supposed to be flying in soon. Everything is normal for your position, everything is decided."

I wanted to shake him.

"Try to understand that I was not born yesterday. I know a few things. I do not want all this jerking around!"

"No, no, everything is normal," he assured me. "Don't worry. Everything will be okay."

"Well, okay, I'll wait."

I waited for Tikhonov for hours, until about 11 p.m.

"Wait for Valentine Kozin," he said. "He is taking care of the matter. He is the leader of the delegation. He has the passports."

I waited for Kozin.

"Igor, your passport is not here," he said. "You are not going."
Well, at least this time they didn't wait until morning to tell me.

I drove along the habitual route home, in my own car. The vagueness of it was oppressive. This was the real torture. Why wouldn't someone tell me what I was supposed to have *done?* No –Larionov had not done anything to be punished for – but let him go abroad? No, no!

And then, suddenly, they began to show touching care about me. They tried not to leave me alone with my own bitter thoughts, nor in the company of my friends for a long time. They began to invite me – no, closer to summon me – for soul-searching discussions, usually held in the political division of the CSRA, or in Glavpur, the head political administration office of the Soviet Army and Navy.

They did not give a damn about hockey or anything connected with it. They had a more important government problem to solve: to expose Larionov!

I had to appear in my military uniform, which was a joke in itself. At that time I was senior lieutenant, and a sorry excuse for one. I had not fired a shot from my pistol even once. I did not know how to disassemble the automatic weapon. The only technique I had mastered was in hockey, the only battle tactics those on ice. The military uniform was too tight. It pinched and confined me, as if made for someone else. It was made for someone who deserved it, who had two years of mandatory military service behind him, someone who had finished his military schooling. This was for show, this changing of the clothes, which was against my nature. Humiliation was in the very procedure of my coming to the authorities.

They suspected me of everything, accused me of everything.
"Did you know, Captain Larionov, that a provocative incident took place in your home?"
I was taken aback. Now the conspiracy was in my own home!
It turned out that they were talking about a visit to the home of my parents by a representative of the Canada-USSR Friendship Society. The representative was a guest of the World Festival of Youth and Students, which was held in Moscow during the summer of 1985. The representative was a Canadian female student who was upset at my absence from the important matches. She visited for half an hour. According to the rules of Russian hospitality, my parents gave her tea.
This was it, if in but a few words.

But, in more detail, it was thus:

The Canadian girl's name was Frances. She was a hockey fanatic. At the Festival she was photographed with Tretiak, and many newspapers gladly printed the picture. Friendship knows no borders! Canada and the USSR are great hockey powers!

Frances' passion for hockey did not subside here. She came to the CSRA, on Leningrad Prospect, to our training rink. It was during the summer, it was hot, when we had only just begun to play. It was either a sparring match with Khimik, or with another team. As an uninvited guest at the rink, she was shown out of the sports complex. Apparently, our rink is considered sacred ground, and impossible for a foreigner to enter just like that.

In order to present her enthusiasm for hockey I will add: it seems that for two years Frances had played goalie for a factory team of Sacco and Vancetti, the pencil company that the American millionaire, Armand Hammer gave to the Soviet republic in 1920.

The Canadian female goalkeeper, according to the word of the guys from the factory, looked like a fine fellow. And as a girl? I was more than calm observing her. She is not my type.

The day after her removal to "the end of the game," Frances drove over to my parents' home see me. Purely by accident (I already had my own one-room place) I happened to be there. I tried to drop in on them at every opportunity. We conversed together around tea. She kept asking why I did not appear in the matches abroad. I could not answer anything sensibly. Soon the Canadian girl left and I completely calmly went about my own business.

This they called a provocative incident?

I was calm, but not entirely, I suppose. Because earlier they had read to me the moral teaching that a Soviet officer does not have the right to be found even three feet from a foreigner, never mind inviting someone home. I remember the incident that happened to Sergei Belov, perhaps one of the best basketball players of the 1970s. He happened to have a foreign guest. After that he was denied travel privileges. So I kept this condition in mind.

All this of course is terrible stupidity. But there I was, in a situation out of a novel by De Maupassant. They had drawn up a connection between the Canadian girl to me, a connection that never existed and, to put it gently, was not encouraged.

It was bizarre. Even at that time, cordial feelings towards foreigners, male or female, were not in themselves criminal. Marriages between Russians and foreigners were registered without protests. Boris Spassky, the former world chess champion, married a French woman and moved to France. But for me, everything appeared differently. I had officer's rank! It gave me knowledge of strategic secrets!

Okay, if I had loved her, then I would not have been so angry at these insults. But I was not in any way taken by Frances. But if I had been taken by a woman, what of it? What limitations can there be for feelings? Is one supposed to love according to instructions? I could have liked a blonde from somewhere around Volga, or a brunette from Japan. What is strange here? Nothing. I am not some kind of robot that can fulfil mindless demands without being involved in where I sit, where I stand, and when I say what. I consider myself a contemporary person. While we are young we must take a few things from life. Isn't that so?

This does not mean at all that I am without principles. I have them in my views on many questions, relationships with women included. And with every year I kept trying to follow more strictly my own personal views, and not yield to the herd instinct.

But I was accused not only of weird adventures with women. As it turned out, they also had something else on me. There in the Glavpur, during the next meeting, they were prepared to nail me to the chair with new undefendable proof of my transgressions:

"According to information in our possession, your mother is involved in speculation."

My mother, they said, was speculating in video equipment and other fast-moving imported goods. You would have to be mad to come to such a conclusion! My mother has never sold anything. And not only did she not sell them for a dear price, nor for their original price – she never had anything to sell! Because you had to have money in the first place to buy the things, and Mama lived on her own hard-earned, piddly eighty rubles a month ($55 CDN). She is from the generation that is used to plowing and sewing from dawn to dusk. Even now, on pension, when she has high blood pressure, she sticks to her furrows in the ground from morning to night. She is a peasant by heart.

This was their accused speculator.

It was easy to deduce the tack they were taking: if Larionov goes abroad, it means that he brings back black market goods to sell. And that's the long and short of it.

Yet there was no such proof that could be brought forward. Allegedly messages were received about a provocation being prepared. My romance with the Canadian girl most likely surfaced at that time. Then, suddenly, they knew what my mother did in her declining years and for the bettering of the family's position! A joke!

But there was more, a veritable bouquet of accusations of various shapes and sizes. At the next audience the members of the Glav-pur brought forth new sketches of my sadly repellent portrait.

"Comrade Senior Lieutenant, you like the West very much. And in general everything from the West."

I was at fault all around. That I gladly gave interviews to journalists. That I liked the NHL, and the organization of the hockey business there. That I like rock music. That the living standard there impressed me. All this was raked up into a pile. I was the enemy. Because, you see, if I liked the American way of life, then in general I was an American by heart. All of this they said about me.

By nature I am clearly a Russian. And I do not like everything in America. It cannot be that somewhere everything is as in a fairy-tale, and somewhere else is total darkness and hopelessness. Particularly, it seemed, my sociability offended the preservers of government secrets and questioners of my reliability. I also knew a little English. Therefore I had the possibility to rub elbows with whomever I might come in contact: hockey players, journalists and even immigrants. And, they assumed, to each of them I could give important information – everyone getting an equal share, no doubt, in order to be fair.

Tikhonov tried to persuade me that he had been there, that he had consulted with them and made requests for my sake. Some sort of support came from him. Verbal support, moral support. But words no longer "cured" me. He kept on trying to calm me.

"Don't worry. We will resolve your question."

But I still didn't understand. What *was* my question?

At press conferences abroad, in the very countries where they supposedly had prepared these terrible traps for me, as though I was a valuable fur-bearing animal, journalists were still curious. They heard the constant hint of my sharply declining health, of colds which knocked me off my feet, as bad luck would have it, just before the very departure gate.

They heard: "Larionov has tonsillitis. His glands are not in order, they are inflamed." Suddenly, I wasn't a hockey player in the prime of life, I was one who was falling apart. Yesterday I played for the championship of the Soviet Union and did not embarrass myself. Today it was a matter of my glands – glands I didn't even know where to locate.

I want to be objective. Tikhonov did show some action. Yes, he supported me. Because he was interested. Directly interested. The first squad was splitting up. The squad which carried the majority of the most responsible matches of the club and of the National team. And the World Championships were upcoming, the championships that were always the main thing in his life.

The coach had an interest in me, all right. I didn't need travel permits to play in the championships. Not this year. This year they were to be played in Moscow. Apparently no one was preparing a provocation against me there.

Danger crept up to me now from another side.

I was deprived of the important playing and practice time of international meetings. It was a wasted season. I either played for the Championship of the Soviet Union, or "rested" while the team, my teammates, went on tour. As always, the CSRA won the championship of the Soviet Union without any problems. And as always this brought quite moderate happiness. We were, after all, three heads higher than all the rest.

Again we get together, preparing for the 1986 World Championship. Trips were also being planned to West Germany and Finland. And, again, I had the same sort of mysterious but already familiar delays.

"Sorry, there is something with your documents..."

Yes, they knew what was going on. No, it didn't occur to them to explain everything humanely.

"You can train here, in Novogorsk, by yourself," Tikhonov told me. "There will be three or four fellows from the reserves of the National team. Or drive with Myshkin to Leningrad. (Myshkin was the goalkeeper who replaced Tretiak on the National team, played in the 1979 Canada Cup and caused a fury when we won it from the hosts, 6-0). You can play there for the second National team representatives in the tournament."

This made sense. In order not to totally lose touch with playing, I chose the second option.

We somehow got through the first and second match. It was so difficult. We were rusty in every aspect. Training or no training, it had been a long time since I really played. Then I found the groove, and felt I was starting to play as normally. I made it to the All-Stars in the tournament of second National teams.

Yuri Ivanovich Moiseev and I had a very good relationship. Human contact. It had been formed in those years when he was assistant coach of the CSRA, with Tikhonov. Moiseev reported to the senior coach of the National team:

"Larionov is in great shape. I am satisfied with his playing."

I had barely stepped off the Leningrad-Moscow train when I

went straight to the Novogorsk base and to the ice for the Nationals' training session. Tikhonov watched and watched and screwed up his face. Larionov, he said, was not ready to play. He then explained it to Yurzinov, then to Fetisov, the captain of the National team, then to my teammates:

"It's a shame he's not ready, but he did not catch on to the rhythm of the game. He held on to the puck too long."

Hockey is not arithmetic. Still, when one specialist says white, and another calls the very same thing black, this causes one to wonder.

But the solution was on the surface. Tikhonov could not forgive his former assistant Moiseev, the assistant who left for a promotion to senior coach of Moscow Dynamo. Therefore, Viktor Vasilevich could not allow it that someone else beside himself would help me to attain my "battle" conditioning. And most definitely not Moiseev! Again, then, my affairs, as they say, were nothing to thank God about.

"Okay," I told myself. "Here, in hockey, I'll somehow sort it out myself. I do not have to wait like a beggar for someone else's explanations."

On the following day a match was held between the first and second National teams, the last scheduled match before the World Championship and the proclamation of those who would take part. In the morning I had been useless, but in this game everything somehow fell into place. I threw a couple into the net. When the list was posted, I was on it. I was back on the top National team. Mind you, we were playing in Moscow and no travel was involved.

Without fail, we had to get back the championship title, lost a year earlier in Prague. A day or two before the beginning of the tournament, Yurzinov sat down next to me after supper.

"Igor, dear Igor," he said. "Now a lot depends on how you play, how we play. Your future depends on it. Whether you will be able to go abroad or not."

This whole story was so repellent to me, all this word play, that I only nodded and kept quiet.

"If we win, then we can go to the top for you," he added persuasively, "to tell them there that we very much need a player."

He left the worst case unsaid: If we lost, don't count on it.

I treated this conversation coolly and was not particularly upset over it. Whether I would be allowed to travel or not, it was all the same. In the end, truth is victorious. Moreover, these were different times in the country. This was 1986. But the renewal was still far from what is desired. In life, unfortunately, much was still showing through from years past, and then the fresh wind of change did not always blow.

Someone, apparently meaning well, confidentially informed me that I would never be allowed to travel abroad. By some sort of long chain, which led almost all the way to the Central Committee of the Communist Party or to the KGB, information was spread which linked me to journalists in the West and what is more, with girls in the West, and therefore the road in a western direction was forbidden to me.

I was not desperate. I found myself in a blind alley, but I did not think of myself as trapped. Somehow, I would get out into the clear light.

The situation was indefinable, in the extreme. But I did not climb the walls because of this. To go to the West was not the criteria of life for me, or to buy something there, to bring it back and place it at home or to sell it for three times its original price. I went there only as a hockey player, as a professional. I brought back video equipment, a camera and other technical equipment, but this was not some aim of mine or the extent of my wishes. If, God forbid, I was not allowed again to travel to Canada or Sweden, I could live without it.

But not being able to go to Canada to Sweden, to Czechoslovakia or West Germany cost me quite a bit more than the simple purchasing of brand name goods. I was losing practical experience. You cannot trade playing time at a high level for anything. A lowering of my elementary hockey skills was threatening me, just as a worker lowers his own standard if they move him from a computerized machine to an ordinary machine. More than anything, this prospect depressed me.

Still, the hope lived with me all the same, that I would be able to return to my own Voskresensk and to play there. Why should I run through the mill in the CSRA, deprive myself of the elementary pleasures of life, and sit me for weeks on end at gatherings without a break only because Tikhonov demands it? Tikhonov, whom I could not stand more and more. Why did I have to? These evermore senseless sacrifices were totally worthless.

There was nothing left for me to do in the CSRA, if I as a member of the National team did not have the right to play any further west than Brest. Such thoughts turned around in my mind and they somehow consoled me. I had a place to go to. I had the opportunity to break out of the vicious circle. I could go home.

If this dawdling drew out further, I would give notice of my departure and go to Voskresensk, even though it meant I would lose the possibility to play on the first squad and hardly get the chance to wear again the uniform of the National team. Such was my reality at that moment.

The season finally ended, and with a World Championship. Everything was wonderful in our hockey! Our hockey was the best in the world!

The cycle began again.

Holidays.

Archangel.

Another season was coming up – 1987.

"Let it be a hockey season," I thought. "Just a hockey season."

The CSRA went to West Germany twice for friendly matches, and four days later into the European Cup championship. Before the first trip I received an injury, a bruised buttock. Just a light injury, I'd have enough time to heal.

The old questions remained: Would I be allowed to travel with the team? If I was not, did it make any sense for me to continue to train with it? I asked for answers. Guess the reply: There were still formalities standing in the way of my travel.

Well, there was one thing I could do, one all-important thing I wanted more than anything else, one thing that did not involve visas or passports or travel.

I could get married.

I could no longer imagine my life without Lena. I was already thinking, that this hallucination must end some day. What reason was there to wait? On the very next day I would make the proposal of marriage.

To marry, to marry. But to marry such as people do, with friends, and relatives. To marry officially. With a sea of flowers, and a river of champagne. A weight was off my shoulders. With all my being, I felt that I had made my choice in life. This would be the main thing in my life, ahead of my hockey.

Usually one has to wait such a long time to register a marriage, to stand in those eternal lines as with everything else. But, here the officials at the Bureau of Statistics met us halfway. They helped us. All the marriage papers were quickly processed.

All the premarriage bustle was pressured to the limit. My head was spinning. The eve of marriage, late at night, we could finally breathe a sigh of relief, be a little calmer. It seemed that everything was thought of, that we had not forgotten anything. And suddenly: Oh, no! For the day that would provide the memories of our lives, we'd forgotten to get a photographer!

I phoned an acquaintance photo correspondent, the number one in the country in the area of sports, the winner of many international competitions, "World Press Photo" among them. Often he had urgently sought me out and taken shot after shot. But when for the first time the need came up for me, a marriage!, I heard:

"Old man, I'm sorry. We have the wife's relatives with us unexpectedly. From Hungary. Tomorrow, I can't."

Another lesson.

Fine. Another photo correspondent saved me, one who we had seen only once before then.

The wedding was on the Aug. 21, 1986. The act of registration was set at 10 a.m. They gave me leave from the training session so that I could be at the palace of matrimony – but insisted I make it back for the evening session at 5 p.m.

But I wanted to get together the parents, friends, and teammates. Slava Fetisov had already during my absence approached Tikhonov and asked that the guys be excused from the base. Roughly half of the team got together in this request. The coach knew the reason why. So he met us halfway. He let them go. However, we couldn't really go all out and celebrate for three days, as the Russians love to do. There was no time.

The day after the wedding, they summoned me to the Central Committee of the Party. They asked me to appear there in the next morning.

Those who had troubled themselves for my sake, all those "military" Red Army officers with ranks of major and higher, zealously instructed me:

"Learn the thesis of the April Plenum of the Central Committee and so on. What if they should suddenly ask you questions, and you won't know anything? You are not just going anywhere, you are going to the Central Committee!"

"What's there to learn?" I told them. "I read the newspapers."

I appeared at the appointed hour. I walked into the office. They met me in a friendly way, as if it had not been me who could not go abroad for half a year, but Ivanov or Sidorov. A man of middle age was the boss of the office.

"Well, Igor, how are things?"

"The usual."

"How are things on the team?"

"Okay. We are preparing for the season."

"Will there be a competition in the Soviet Union this season?"

"Not really. Hardly. The CSRA is heads above everyone else..."

And that was the whole conversation!

Nothing about the weird provocations, which had to do with me, nor anything of the kind about my offenses, nothing about the April Plenum – not even half a word.

Why did they summon me? For the sake of formality.

On the next day, instead of setting out on my honeymoon, I went to the customs control office at Sheremetevo airport. After a half-year interval, I flew out with the team to West Germany!

The same officials who suspected me in God knows what sins, and other officials also, greeted me after the tournament in West Germany as a hero! For the sake of the order of things, they cheered my success in those matches of little importance.

"Congratulations on your victory!" they cooed, strongly shaking my hands and patting me on the back, beaming like a clean Tula samovar, a sincere, radiant shine in their eyes. "Thank you! We believed in you! You didn't let us down!"

I could barely stand it.

"Excuse me," I asked, "but why are you saying these things?"

"We believed in you. And you returned to the Motherland."

How could this be taken as anything but a cruel insult? Here again, you see, I was now justifying someone else's hopes. I'd gone to the West – and returned to the Soviet Union! Did this mean I was finally considered trustworthy?

Neither in my dreams, nor in my heart had I suspected that I would become the author of a sensation in such a manner – although admittedly a sensation only in the lobbies and offices of the Central Committee.

This detective story was finishing so awkwardly and humiliatingly. If I had wanted, if I had tried to move to the West, is it not possible that I would have found the time and place? Every year I had loads of opportunities for such a serious step. And when, again and again, I did not take it, should not that have shown that I lacked any irresistible desire towards everything of the West?

And in general, what kind of a question is that: Will he return or not?

A man has the right to live where he wants to. On the whole, during those months when I found myself denied travel privileges and placed under every kind of suspicion, I probably thought over and experienced more than in all my previous years of major hockey.

As the storm clouds dispersed from over my head, they took with them many illusions I had held up to then. It became as clear as two times two is four: in this complex life which I myself had chosen, I could depend on my own will above all, my own head, my own principles. I had to be ready to answer for any action, even for those which I did not commit.

They say that experiences harden you. And so they did. After all of this slander, suspicion, and accusations; after I had carried on myself the label "denied travel privileges", after powerless attempts to prove that I was right, I had not become weaker. Actually, I had become stronger spiritually. I understood this significantly later, when new, serious experiences emerged in my life – experiences by no means related to the plan of hockey.

But after that, as I justified the hopes of the colonels from sports CSRA, indeed a new life began for me. Beside me now was Lena, my wife. Family life was a joy for me. Soon we began to wait for the appearance of Alyonka.

All the people who'd been around me earlier, until the misfortune, remained on my horizon. But now I viewed many of them as if through high-power binoculars.

A lot of people whirled around me before this wrongful accusation – whirled somewhere beside me, called me up, shook hands, earnest about something they were asking. They did not hesitate to ask for a stick with an autograph, to invite me out to restaurants. Those people, from then on, I regarded categorically as spongers. Their ranks melted away like snow under a March sun, with every new occurrence of Larionov being denied travel privileges. I know that they enthusiastically whispered behind my back about what I might have done to deserve this. The black market! Currency speculation! Aha, again Larionov is not in the body of the team going abroad. It cannot be for any other reason than that he has again done something seriously wrong. People are not just simply denied travel privileges...

They lost interest in me as a person. But I had always treated their servile hum calmly, and now, when justice had triumphed after all, and these same people tried to retrace their steps, their hypocrisy was already visible to me. It flew in my face. I was sick of it.

They, of course, understood that they turned out to be wrong. But the public is an interesting lot. It was like water off a duck's back to them. They changed like weathercocks and again sang the old tunes as they circled around me. But I could no longer forgive. They were not even friends before, people whom I would have trusted. I simply increased the distance between us. I did not say anything, did not explain, but there was a coldness in my voice, with my tone, my looks, that let them know that we were by no means going the same way.

But those who had been friends remained such. Friends, the real ones, became 10 times more dear to me. There were not many of them. But you don't need many, if they are genuine. Without friends, is it really possible to live?

With my teammates, it was more complex.

I had absolutely nothing to reproach them for. Later from the position of passed years and the sharpest conflicts with Tikhonov, and the line scattered through the NHL, I would analyze their behavior rather easily.

My linemates themself had been perplexed. They did not understand what was happening. They also worried about me. At that time, I think, a person could not be found who would be able to unite the remaining four into a fist, into a nucleus that could stand as one in my defense. However, it was very, very complex. Their self-consciousness, and mine also, made it more difficult. Those who ran hockey had placed under doubt the return of the dispatcher of the squad to the Motherland from any foreign tour. They suspect him of preparing to immigrate. But the teammates, true and longstanding, magnificent masters and hockey warriors, knew perfectly well that all of this was absolute gibberish.

Slava Fetisov was always among us as a leader, the head on the ice. We went through thick and thin for him. Ideologically, it was Fetisov who could have organized my defense, if you will, of honor and worthiness. For even off the ice Viacheslav was a direct and courageous man. An individual. But there was no one who could analyze the situation and unite the remaining players.

I do not have a grain of blame for anyone, not for Fetisov, nor Makarov, nor Krutov, who were less initiative. Kasatonov, in general, was not one of those who would risk his personal well-being or career for the sake of someone else,

If such a situation befell one of them, could I take upon myself the role of defender? Then, in 1985? It is hard to say. One thing I know for sure: I would not remain completely silent. For I had expressed my own point of view, sharply different from the officially permitted one, already in 1984, in Canada, publicly.

I have already admitted that during the day one can dream up such nonsense, such abracadabra with some sort of burdensome shades, that you later discover with joy, ah, this, thank God, it did not happen in reality!

Would it not be correct to say, then, that this whole story of my being denied travel privileges is similar to the flight of mosquitos through the clouds in the hour after lunch?

Maybe that is why I now stay awake during this hour. And why I do not consider this at all as a bad omen.

Chapter 8
BOMBSHELL

On an early Moscow morning in October, 1988, people around the street kiosks picked up issue No. 42 of the popular magazine OGONYOK, read in wonder pages 18 and 19, and shook their heads. Even those who had no interest in major sports knew that Igor Larionov would be in big trouble for this.

"What will happen to him now?" they asked one another. They did not know, exactly, but they knew it wouldn't be pleasant. Because I had done the unthinkable. I had written a sensational article in the press, an open letter that sharply criticized the hockey system in which I worked. And for this I would have to pay...

I always regarded the press with close attention, reading what caught my interest and giving interviews both in the U.S.S.R. and abroad. But in my wildest dreams I never saw myself as an author of an article that would produce such a commotion.

I am a hockey player, and only a hockey player. This is my profession, my favorite work, and I would not change it for anything. I had never given journalism a thought. So it is curious to churn over again the events which led up to the writing of my open letter in OGONYOK. A step so unusual and decisive, so loaded with serious consequences, was not taken with only an hour of thought.

So, what did all this begin with? With the flow of time, how did I mature to lay out this journalistic bomb? In a sense I suppose you could say the seed was planted that day in 1981 when I arrived at the CSRA and grew all those years as my opinion worsened of my immediate superiors who, thanks to their unlimited power, seemed to cover my horizons. My situation grew steadily worse and appeared hopeless --but there was Tikhonov, inflexible, unbending and seemingly untouchable.

But there was a sequence to it, high points (or, rather, low) to which I can put a date.

September 1984. It began here, I believe, with the interviews given North American correspondents during the Canada Cup matches. I said what I thought. I expressed my own opinion – which I had not discussed with anyone previously – about the NHL, about Soviet-Canadian contact, about many things. As I have already said, I did not have to wait long for the consequences. This was the starting block for my open perception of hockey and everything connected with it.

November 1985. As always, we were living under lock and key at the country base in Archangel, connected with the outside world only by that single telephone in the hall on the first floor.

But we had the television, and the press. And the rumour spread: someone had written a daring article in a journal about our hockey – sharply and objectively, without the usual glorification, based on the National team's bad luck at the World Championship in Prague. Soon after the tournament, material with the claim of being critical had been published, but did not touch the real story. But now – where could we get hold of this magazine? Finally, one copy appeared at the base. We read it in turns.

The headline was: **"The Long Echo of the Season."** The author, journalist Leonid Reizer, could not have expected that this echo would last so long and be so loud. The guys – I have in mind Fetisov, Krutov, and Makarov – read the article with interest and obvious approval. I reread the article twice.

Above all, the very fact, that a journalist dared to criticize Tikhonov attracted my attention. Tikhonov himself! But further, it was important that this criticism argumentatively exposed the hockey monarch who ruled our game and whose unhealthy eyes glared at our players like the barrels of two huge pistols. What is it I remember about this publication? That I was in agreement with it, and could not add to the mass of facts and reasons.

I understood also that people like Reizer who understood hockey or participated in it were putting themselves at risk in being opposed to the established order of things. Nonetheless, it roused in me a still secret desire, to be in print at some time.

Some day...

December 1985 to August 1986. During these extremely long months, when I was unable to travel abroad, I matured quickly. I had a strong feeling within me of displeasure with the management of our hockey, of the conditions under which I had to directly work. An inner protest began to gain strength.

December 1987: Reizer, correspondent of the popular magazine

SOCCER-HOCKEY and the author of that first article, suggested that we meet.

"Let's calmly talk together," he said. "We will talk about what worries you, worries me, and worries all hockey lovers."

I agreed. More, I viewed the discussion as a possible piece for publication, particularly if the talk went as had that first article. I'd seen the flow of truth about the history of our country, hard and dismal, gushing forth in the embassy newspapers and journals. I wanted fairness to touch the sports and hockey press, to bring the problems to light and perhaps to solve some of them through exposure to the light. Here seemed an opportunity.

"Well, okay, we'll discuss a bit, objectively," I said. "But will they publish it? Wouldn't what was left (after editing and/or censoring by the magazine) be but a pitiful bit?"

Leonid assured me:

"Igor, I, no less than you, want to stir up our hockey swamp, naming things in your name. I cannot give you a guarantee, but if they start to cut something from your interview, to shorten it, to correct it for fear of injuring someone, I strongly promise you that I will myself remove it. I will not publish merely for publication's sake."

They published the interview. I liked it. I liked it a lot. I would not say that I told him everything that had occurred or that had been building up inside of me. But Leonid kept his promise, the editorial management loyally conducted itself (to everyone's surprise), and the grains of truth concerning hockey were truthfully and successfully told.

The weekly magazine comes out on Sundays. By Tuesday, I was publicly taken back into the ranks by writers, who now all wanted to discuss these things with me. At the meeting of the National team, Tikhonov roared with all his might:

"Comrades, I always thought that I was working with hockey players. But here, do you understand, it has become clear that I was not right. Among us are *writers!* Larionov, for example, is a Boris Pasternak!"

I think we could safely say he was not pleased.

February 1988. In Calgary, in the heat of the Winter Olympics, they arranged a hockey press conference where for some reason they invited me. I was without a translator, but I understood the first question perfectly:

"Mister Larionov, what changes have occurred in Soviet hockey after your interview in the December issue of SOCCER-HOCKEY?"

I answered frankly.

"I do not hope for some kind of large and speedy change for the better," I said. "Little time has passed, and it is time that all was centred on the preparation for the Games. But, I am not losing hope. We shall see what we shall see."

March 1988. Oh, the promises Tikhonov made us just before the Olympic matches! First things first! Fate would smile on us if we obtained the championship for ourselves and for him! Then there would be more freedom and independence, a reduction in the duration of the National team camps, more time at home with our families!

In Goskomsport, not without Tikhonov's knowledge, I suppose, they promised us that the question of our appearance in the NHL would be resolved in the very near future. But already winter had turned to spring, we had won the gold medal – and everything remained as it was. What then was the value of the coach's assurance? There were still three days until the next unremarkable match, but there we were, whiling away the time in Archangel. As always.

I broke curfew and spent a short night in a grill bar "Veterok", only a hundred metres from the base. At the table opposite me was a Canadian correspondent who was writing a book about Soviet hockey. Beside me sat the dejected Krutov, who was fed up with this damn National team no less than I. The cassette of the Canadian's dictaphone recorded my words, which came forth as if on their own.

A thought flashed through my mind: Why was I saying all this now, about that which is not published in the Soviet Union?

July 1988. Slava Fetisov had to be the first to conclude a contract with a club in the NHL. He was very interested in the New Jersey Devils, who had selected him in the league draft in the hope that some arrangement could be made – as Calgary had selected Makarov and Vancouver had picked Krutov and myself. The three of us were to follow him across the ocean in a year.

Therefore, we were particularly interested in how the affair developed for our captain. From the beginning they promised him, at a sufficiently high level, that there would not be a problem. And then the red tape began.

No one said anything in earnest. Negotiations with the Devils stopped. He was in a suspended state, in limbo. Three times the New Jersey management flew halfway across the world, and returned from Moscow without anything.

You would not wish it on an enemy. Especially not on Slava, who is my friend. It was painful to look at him, irritated, disappointed by the word that had been given him, grown tired from going from office to office, lost.

One did not have to be so bright to conclude that the red tape was placed by the all-respected Viktor Vasilevich Tikhonov. With the cult of personality established in our hockey around this specialist, the question of concluding the first contract between a Soviet hockey player and a club from the NHL could hardly take place without first discussion with Tikhonov. I could easily imagine the same tape binding me in a year, when negotiations began with the representatives of the Canucks. Without fail, Krutov and Makarov were also thinking about this.

August 1988. During a two-week and completely useless training camp for the candidates of the National team, I visited Tikhonov with a request:

"Allow me to live at home. I will train, only I will not spend the night at the base."

And again I heard a refusal, covered with a promise which I had not believed for a long time. "No Igor, now I cannot but refuse," he said. "This is the first time we are gathering the candidates. But we'll find you some spare time off, so that it will be possible for you to while away at home."

It was inconceivable. In *August* it was a life and death necessity for me to spend the night at the base? Well, the World Championship was not far off. Only eight months! This small, empty episode was the drop which finally overflowed the cup of my patience.

Early September 1988. I was back in the coach's room – but this time, not as a visitor with a request. In the presence of his assistant, Mikhailov, I made an announcement to Tikhonov:

"This is it. I am playing my last season in the CSRA!"

Tikhonov hardly believed my words. Mikhailov advised me to calm down and not to hurry. I kept going:

"I am finally satisfied that nothing will change here. All things will remain as they are. So, that is my decision, finally. I have let you know in advance."

Mid-September 1988. Glasnost had penetrated into the sports arena. Earlier, the writer's brotherhood had mostly passed me by. Now, suddenly, I was in great demand. The fan poll by the weekly SOCCER-HOCKEY had recognized me as the best player in the country for the past season. Various publications were being prepared for the first-person interview and others about me.

Remarkable. Without the award, this could not have happened. But I wondered about something else. The previous June I had been interviewed by the editorial journal SPORTS GAMES. The article had never appeared. I phoned the editor and asked when it was planned.

"We are planning it for the December issue," I was told.

To wait so long? Why? And here a friend and journalist advised:

"If you want to have your thoughts and words published without reservation and read by the most people, go to OGONYOK. You will not find a better publication today! Besides, circulation of SPORTS GAMES is 150,000, which is miserly for a huge country."

I went to OGONYOK! Here, finally, splashing full speed ahead from under the press, would roar the stream that had been pent up inside me over the years.

The magazine officials were divided on this offer from, as they called me, "The most battling pen." But a correspondent vindicated his own reputation. We agreed to begin work on the material. But I remembered the delaying tactics of SPORTS GAMES. This time I asked, and was assured the article would appear in the very next issue, in mid-October.

This was class!

We decided that it would be in the form of an open letter from Igor Larionov to the coach Viktor Tikhonov. I, for some reason, trusted this unknown correspondent, and did not think that another meeting would be necessary. Still, on the appointed day, as he read the finished product to me over the phone after the morning training session, I stopped talking when people approached. In this, superfluous ears were not needed.

It came out better than I had hoped for. The main point was that I, Larionov, had informed Tikhonov, one-on-one, that I had played my last season for CRSA.

I made the jump. "Let's put it in!" I told him.

I was not in Moscow when issue number 42 of OGONYOK appeared. The CSRA team was playing a match at the European Cup Championship in Switzerland. But I'm told that sports-minded Moscow buzzed literally like a beehive.

"Have you heard Larionov is in OGONYOK?"

My open letter began this way:

"Dear respected Viktor Vasilevich!

"For the last six years, from that very day of our particularly personal, intimate discussion (when) you made it known at the general meeting of the team that you blamed me for a 'weak game,' we have been in no way successful in speaking with you sincerely. Such a situation did not present itself although we worked together..."

There is no sense to bring in more excerpts from the letter. Several concerned the myth surrounding Tikhonov and the methods he mercilessly used to support his formula that "for the achievement of goals, all means are good."

I began with the business of inviting players from all over the country, and the manner in which the talented ones were transformed into instant military officers, and recalled the manner in which I unexpectedly became a lieutenant. I outlined the way the players' sports fate and their futures were controlled, and the way in which they were kept from their families, all with the aim of placing them under the absolute control of the senior coach.

"So you, Viktor Vasilevich, have become transformed in the last years into this hockey monarch: you punish who you want, you pardon who you want! How you accosted Sasha Mogilny, the very youngest player, when he did not wish to become an officer in the Red Army. An old Cossack method: having scared him, you did not take him to the exhibition game in Japan. And they pondered, what is wrong with you. And Sasha obediently wrote the report (joined the army)"

I am not a prophet. I did not imagine the dramatic turning point in the fate of Alexander Mogilny – that within six months of this publication he would defect to join the NHL Buffalo Sabres. I do not think the article and Mogilny's understanding of it were an essential point in influencing his action. The surroundings, the situation on the team, the insidious appointment to officer's rank, which amounted to enslaving the player – all these things and his own character combined to push him to the decision to leave. I could not avoid bringing out those things which continually annoyed me.

"For 10 months of the year we were forced to be separated from home: endless trips, games, and if not games then training camps. A harsh regime. Listing what was allowed us was easy: There was a lot that we could do. They nursed us wonderfully well. We could play chess or cards, and we could sleep. All else that remained for us to do was to train. After the game we were on the bus. Our wives and kiddies waved us "goodbye." They are going home, thanks to you, Viktor Vasilevich! (It's amazing) *how our wives could give birth to our children* (considering the training schedule). *These normal, mutual relationship between a hockey player and his wife, do not have a part in your program."*

In reality this system of the National team was accepted in all clubs. The problem itself had a common sound. But in the CSRA, thanks to the army subordination and the character of the senior coach, all was taken to a higher, utterly unacceptable level. I adhere to the emotional perception of the game. Mood, the outer composition of the player and the team as a whole, all determine the outcome of the battle. And those training camps drove a weird anxiety into everyone.

"The athlete's life in Soviet hockey is short. On the eve of a series of championships, the composition of the National team is announced in the newspapers and fans write letters. 'Where are our famous stars?' they ask. 'Are they really trying so hopelessly that they can not even go out onto the ice?' Why did Vladislav Tretiak, the most popular Soviet hockey player in the world, leave the game at 32? The answer is simple. They would not allow Tretiak, even in view of his exceptionalness, to prepare for the games on his own, at home."

In the structure of Soviet sport only Goskomsport of the USSR and the directors of the administration of soccer and hockey of Kolosky are higher than the CSRA and Tikhonov. Here you would expect recognition of the Tikhonov-esque methods, the senselessness and humiliation of the plan as it was used by the senior coach. But no.

"So, from year to year you trained people as if they were pawns in your hands. You must think that in Goskomsport they also do not rack their brains very much about the psychological preparation of sportsmen. Here, Viktor Vasilevich, you use influence and immense respect: From time to time you give Goskomsport results. 'He won the latest World Championship! Thank you, comrade Tikhonov, for your work!'"

Then came the lines that appeared in the opening of this book, the exposure of the injections and drug test cheating that were the article's knockout punch in the eyes of the foreign press.Who considers this a loss? And who will answer for it?

Two other quotes from the article require no commentary:

"...life itself shows and proves that your training style, which probably gave positive results in the past, covered the shortcomings, stopped to justify itself, bursting at the seams (like) the very adminis-

tration team system placed in this country. Already you will not be able to hide from anyone; it is seen by everyone – even by Goskomsport, which still silently waited it out because we were still involved at a tournament – that you made mistake after mistake."

And:
"The last years we won on account of good physical conditioning. But, today, other teams of the world go out onto the ice showing endurance, able to maintain a high tempo of the game that was imposed on them. In a word, you can no longer impress anyone with biceps alone."

My open letter closed this way:

"The country is learning to think in a new way, It is high time to take this upon yourself, sportsmen!"

The reaction was instantaneous. Our telephone was white hot and Lena, tired of asking and answering, answering and asking, periodically disconnected it. From everywhere the outcry came, sometimes in a wild form. I could hear the reaction to my article wherever I was, in a store, or at a gas station. Not everyone agreed. On a television broadcast devoted to the problems in sports, one announcer stated that "It is clear that the author of this article is not in good health."

My life, nevertheless, went down the same old narrow path: CSRA, the base in Archangel, training camp, matches. I had more or less anticipated the coach's reaction and that of the club's management from the Major and higher ranks. The reaction of my hockey colleagues was something at which I could only guess, and hope.

A short time before the appearance of OGONYOK, I told my teammates in the squad about the preparations for publication. They had a lively interest:
"What will it be about?"
I only answered:
"When it appears, read it."
It was not because I did not trust them. It was simply that I myself could still not imagine it as a finished product. Still, I wanted the guys to be familiar with the tone of it.

When it appeared and they'd read it, Fetisov firmly shook my hand: "Well done, Igor!" he said. At this time he had problems of his own, but had to feel happy that I would be a public ally in the battle against all this bureaucratic machinery, against the obsolete order of things, against Tikhonov's dictates.

Not surprisingly, for we had discussed it between ourselves more than once, Fetisov, Krutov and Makarov were completely in solidarity with me.

"Everything in the article is right," they said. "Everything written is as it is in life."

But Kasatonov disagreed.

"Hey, you and I are not going the same path," he said. "I do not want to serve somewhere in Khabarovsk! To me, Moscow is not bad. And in general, I think that all this should have been done by other means."

By what means exactly, he did not say. But his talk about the prospects of a military transfer to Khabarovsk drove the final wedge between us. The alienation between us strengthened with every year. His stand at such a complex moment cancelled the bits of friendship still left at that time. After that, he ceased being a person for me. In that thought, I finally lost respect for him.

What kind of team was the CSRA? About 10 people were experienced and had championship titles. But the rest were young and still didn't know anything about hockey life. The experienced players supported the team in various ways. Khrutov, Bykov and Kamensky were supportive to me, if not verbally – not only immediately after the appearance of the article, but on through to my dismissal from the army. Only Kasatonov appeared openly opposed to me. Again, fine. Every wilful person has an opinion. He led such arguments, and that is the main point.

The defenceman Seryozha Starikov was on my side. By spring his wife grew bolder so that in the respectable newspaper SOVIET CULTURE she wrote a letter which spoke about the family life of Soviet hockey stars.

Gusarov, Stelnov? It had been whispered to me that both were for me, and were prepared to sign any article or appeal. We repeated over and over again that we wanted better conditions. But when it became clear that something was promised to them materially – for one an apartment, for another a car – their words, in some conditionally sincere, weren't erased, exactly. They simply lost their strength.

The players from the other clubs? I saw them in passing, and I was not known to them all. But by looks during the usual greetings and handshaking during meetings, I felt some warmth, a sense of solidarity.

Hockey authorities?

"Ivan the Terrible" was the name given to our legendary defencemen of the 1950s, Ivan Tregubov. Formally he did not work in hockey, but he understood this matter, and in the course of it knew what was happening. At one meeting, he ardently lifted up his arms and said in a fatherly way:

"Thanks to you, Igor, for what you have written, so that everything is now in the open. You were the first to write the truth!"

And Semenych? Epstein, of course, immediately reacted. Moreover he himself actively took part in the central press with criticism of Tikhonov's methods. Yury Baulin, having at one time trained with the popular team Spartak, spoke approvingly. The reaction of Anatoly Vladimirovich Tarasov, who knows the whole hockey world, I know from someone else's words: he approved of the publication.

But, what about Tikhonov himself?

For two or three days after the return from Switzerland, Viktor Vasilevich appeared groggy. He did not appear on the ice during the training sessions. Always, when I saw him from afar, he was phoning someone or being phoned. He seemed to be limping. At this moment, without explanation, he announced the boycott. A total boycott. To me, to my face, he did not say more than a word, neither bad nor good. He did not analyze how, in his view, I had lost my way. All matters to me concerning the team on a daily basis were relayed through two assistants.

Fine with me. The less I saw or heard him, the calmer I became.

Public reaction? Autograph seekers surrounded me after every match in greater numbers than before. Where before the OGONYOK letter they would ask me about the match just concluded, strictly hockey questions, now they piled on questions of a completely different nature:

"Igor, is this really all true, what you have written?"

"What is this happening with our hockey?"

"When will they be able to keep Tikhonov in check? Geez, he's become conceited!"

"Igor, aren't you afraid now some unpleasantries await you, eh?"

These retorts, these momentary exchanges with people viewing things from the outside, served as positive feedback to the outcry to my article. I fought back the emotion. They were as breaths of fresh air.

Quickly the CSRA left for the tournament in the Urals. The arenas there are tiny, still of old construction, absolutely not indicative of the colossal popularity of hockey there, from which so many have entered hockey as "naturals". (Makarov, Bykov and Starikov were all from the area.) But there is one advantage in the local arenas: the spectators' rows begin immediately behind the players' bench. You can literally feel the reaction of the fans.

The fans are direct people, workers. During the entire match against the local Tractor team they would bring hands to their mouths and shout:

"Hey, Tikhonov, do you have enough to rob the Urals?"

"Tikhonov, you have completely ruined our hockey!"

Viktor Vasilevich was flabbergasted by such an unregal reception. He lost his bearings and for several moments turned his back to the ice and began a verbal wrangle with the foremost offender. To witness this was quite funny. In the minutes of respite, while sitting on the bench, I heard all this, feeling a certain personal participation of my own for what was happening.

Two days later we played in Sverdlovsk, two hours from Moscow for two games in four days (by Russian hockey standards, a long road trip). Misfortune, they say, comes to smooth ground. In Sverdlovsk, it was my misfortune to prove it.

I was breaking along the boards with the puck, ready to trigger the attack when my legs gave out and I crashed to the ice. The quality of the ice in the Sverdlovsk arena left much to be desired. (Everywhere, quality is the worry of our economy). My skate had hit a crack. It was as if someone had cut me down with a scythe. I felt a sharp pain in the left leg. Two rivals chose the moment to fall on me and make it worse. Diagnosis: fractured right ankle.

The timing of the injury couldn't have been worse. Injuries for a hockey player are a common occurrence. But I had to return to form more quickly than would be considered usual. The ankle injury had given Tikhonov an excuse to take vengeance on me. For the longest time I was not included on the team, and the Super Series tournament in Canada was not that far off.

At first, people decided that I wasn't playing because my enemies were keeping me off the ice after my article in the press. Then, after information was given to the central newspaper, IZVESTIA, on the actual reasons for my absence, one of the players joked with more than a touch of bitterness that "Tikhonov has the evil eye." It was nothing more than coincidence. I had avoided serious injuries, but here, when my life was becoming more complicated, this one had to hit me.

But to repeat the saying, there is no bad without good. I lived at home with my leg in a plaster cast, enjoying the family bustle and playing with Alyonka. I did not have to see the coach, which was good. One sighting and my mood would deteriorate terribly.

Journalists did not forget about me. They arranged something similar to a press conference. I was interested in our press, our radio and television, and in foreign correspondents who were accredited to the capital. My letter in OGONYOK was translated and discussed ardently in many countries of the world. Later, in the middle of winter, a superior of the soccer and hockey management of Goskomsport, Vyacheslav Ivanovich Koloskov, returned from the youth World Championship of soccer in Saudi Arabia and told me, "I read your article there!"

Tikhonov had been quiet, but he had not forgotten. He avenged himself with a deliberate command.

I was already training to the limit with the reserves of the CSRA. Every day I was gaining more of my form. The team doctor informed the coach that I was completely recovered and there was no medical reason not to use me. I tried to take part in the December IZVESTIA tournament. The tournament itself did not attract me, it was just something that was there, the prestige of the tournament was very moderate. I keenly waited for some serious practical playing time. Otherwise, how could I be ready to go to Canada for the Super Series?

The question emerged: Was Tikhonov avenging himself on the author of the infamous open letter, or not? He could scarcely have devised a more convenient opportunity. All it would take was a simple "You know yourself, after the serious injury that Larionov suffered, that he is not ready to do battle with the Canadians from the NHL."

The answer came swiftly. I was not included in the body of the team for the IZVESTIA tournament.

I wasn't surprised. Inside, I'd prepared myself. I'd kept some miserly illusions in relation to Tikhonov's decency. Now they vanished, all at one go. The IZVESTIA was not the issue. What mattered was what was to follow. What would he do about the Super Series roster? I had a sinking feeling that I knew the answer.

For the hockey professional, playing a series of matches in Canada is always an event for which to yearn. There is no more severe test of one's mastery and character. Character is the primary thing. Because this is a holiday for the hockey players. A holiday which does not bore, even if you've experienced it before.

And there was not a hope in hell that I would be going there, to the birthplace of hockey. By agreement with the directors of the NHL, the Moscow club could strengthen with players from other clubs. It made it so easy for the senior coach to punish me further without question, to deprive me of the holiday, the $300 to $350 for the tournament appearance (the promise was for more, but never was it kept) and the prestigious experience. Because he could compensate by taking on players from other clubs.

I did not appear on the unpublished internal list, used for the distribution of new clothes before a foreign tournament. (What is curious and characteristic is that this list concerned only civilian clothes. The quality of our hockey gear – low quality uniforms and equipment that was nothing less than a breach of elementary sports safety, given the potential dangerous nature of our profession – worried only a few.) I will not say that panic grabbed me. I thought, maybe all this confusion accelerated my move back to Voskresensk and Khimik.

Besides, there was another parallel issue at question in those December days. I expected Tikhonov's revenge. But I was not getting ready to give up without a fight. The position, however, became so complicated that I myself did not have the power to influence the move of events. All my hope was on my comrades, Fetisov, Krutov, and Makarov.

And they seemed to be standing on the sidelines, doing nothing.

If you repeated over and over again to me, after OGONYOK came out, your complete solidarity with my point of view and position, I would have said to prove it not with words, but with deeds. "Help me to the end!" I'd say. "Until now I have been fighting all by myself."

The passivity of my teammates left me with a feeling of bewilderment. I was both exasperated and disappointed – a spiritual torment, to be disappointed in those with whom I had done and shared so much over such a long time.

I decided to go to Novogorsk, to the centre for the preparation for the Olympics, where the National team lived during the IZVESTIA tournament. I would go an have a chat with the guys about this and that, at the same time to try to determine their mood.

The weather was wintry, snowflakes piled up into drifts around the camp at Novogorsk, a light frost crunching underfoot. All around it was quiet, clear winter air. I felt like a new arrival, like some sort of boorish fan. I couldn't go into the two-storey building, which housed hockey players in winter and soccer players in summer, because I didn't want to meet up with Tikhonov. But I saw the guys and yes, they talked very well with me. Fetisov Makarov and Krutov worried about me, but they had no doubt what was happening: The coach was having his revenge. It was unfair, but...

I drove home along the Leningrad highway. I felt like shouting. "Where are your friends in a time of trouble? *WHERE???* Can I expect sympathy from you, and nothing more?"

At home, by habit, I tried to mask my feelings. Clearly, the attempt was unsuccessful. My wife understood my despair.

We were at breakfast when the call came from Novogorsk, bringing the answer to those inner questions on the highway the night before. It was Fetisov.

"We three signed a petition to the representative of the All Union Federation," he said. "It says we think that Larionov is ready for the trip to Canada, that the squad needs him, the team needs him. We ask for his inclusion onto the team. Otherwise we will have to think over our personal roles in the tour."

My friends had made their stand. They had issued an ultimatum – an ultimatum to Tikhonov.

It could be viewed in no other way. The rest of the Federation members, who ideologically should have somehow influenced events in hockey life, either did not have any influence at all, or did not wish for extra worries they would receive if they sidestepped any principled actions.

No, this was for Tikhonov. It meant: Either you, Viktor Vasilevich, shut yourself up and order a ticket to Montreal for Larionov, or you will be left without the best defenceman in the world of hockey and the present captain of the team, and also without two wingers who are recognised in the world as superstars. To put it briefly, you will be without a squad for which you have toiled, and which has brought you many dividends.

According to some who were there, Viktor Vasilevich was not himself through that day, and sat the night away in the bathhouse, holding council with the flexible, sensible Koloskov. The next morning Boris Mikhailov phoned me.
phoned me.

"Igor, quickly get ready to leave."

This was a victory, and something more important: My friends had not let me down. I no longer felt along on the battle field, fighting the essential orders of our hockey. Together, we had forced the dictator to retreat for, as far as I knew, the first time in his life.

But he retreated grinding his teeth and warning my friends and protectors who had brought the matter to a head.

"Take into account," he snarled. "For any one of your faults now, I will take a pound of flesh!"

But, in Canada Tikhonov went on as before, as though nothing had happened. And for me, it was as though an evil year grabbed hold of me and would not let go.

In the first match with the Quebec Nordiques, I again received an injury from a seemingly innocent play. Krutov was pushing forward with the puck on the left side. I was laying back, waiting for the attack to develop. There was a sudden, sharp pain in my back, and I was face down on the ice. One of the Nordiques had hit me from behind with his stick. The blow landed in an area practically unprotected. With better equipment, perhaps, but not with what we were wearing. Our own pants had for some reason not arrived. We had to borrow an old set from a nearby school team. Naturally, it did not fit.

The guys carried me to the bench. Our team "doctor" was Igor Silin, a man completely under the thumb of Tikhonov. You might call him a specialist. His speciality: using any means possible to return the injured player to the ice. The health of the player is not serious! Who worries about it?

After the freezing – that unique, all purpose hockey cure – and two or three missed shifts, I was back in the game. I wasn't thinking about the injury, or even my health. My only thought was to prove that I was back in shape, to myself and to the coach. The game was on Soviet television. I couldn't let the people down, or the guys who had taken my side.

I played, and kept playing. But with every match my health grew worse.

I know my own body. I've always been interested in the medical means to care for it. But here, I did not understand what happened. After all those months on a special training program, I'd taken one hit and now I was panting within seconds of going on the ice.

But I didn't tell anyone, particularly the "doctor". Better to endure the pain than than to find myself off the roster for the remaining games of the tour. It would be giving Tikhonov the trump card. I could hear him saying it:

"You see, as I said – Larionov was not ready. He got himself into a mess and received an injury."

Oh, no! I wouldn't give him his wish. He wasn't going to turn everything upside down. No matter what, I would play. And I did, and when the tournament was over I stood third on the team in points, having played 5 1/2 of the six matches – all with a cracked rib.

Tikhonov did not mention this in the interview after the tournament, nor anything about me.

I was not surprised. "Let it be," I told myself. "It will be on his conscience." And it hadn't hurt nearly as much as all that had gone before.

Obviously, that part of it was not over. During the two weeks in Canada I finally gave up any hope that any sort of change would take place on the team where I and half the leading stars and superstars of world hockey had to work. Tikhonov did not change one iota after issue 42 of OGONYOK. If possible, he became even worse.

It was perhaps the darkest moment of all the months of struggle: All the fear and personal risk seemed for nothing. I no longer believed I could win.

Chapter 9
SLAVA

No one was received with such pomp in Canada as Fetisov at the end of December 1980, and at the beginning of 1987. And you should have seen the commotion in New Jersey when we were playing against their home team!

The Devils had drafted Fetisov four years earlier in hope that he might some day become available. And now here he was, perhaps the greatest defenceman on the international stage – saying in numerous interviews in Canada and the U.S. that he no longer planned to play for the CSRA, that he wanted to come to the NHL.

Cameras and reporters followed him everywhere. The interviews were endless. Compliments flew. It was Slava's day, and I was happy for my colleague and friend. Slava is a straightforward man, ever ready to stake everything on his beliefs. Which was precisely what he was doing then, throwing down this challenge to Tikhonov and the CSRA, saying that he wanted to leave.

I understand him perfectly well. He'd signed his contract with the Devils six months earlier, and been put through an emotional wringer ever since, not knowing when or if he'd be allowed to leave. He was humilated, spent. He was now determined to force the issue, no matter what the cost.

We'd barely returned from Canada when an extensive interview appeared in a Moscow youth newspaper. The headline left no doubts: **"Viacheslav Fetisov: 'I don't want to play on Tikhonov's team!'"** On the battlefield outside of hockey there was a new fighting force on the side of the players. And what a force. Fetisov! I could not but be happy about this. He had not discussed his plan to write such an article, any more than I had back in October. But now I had gained reliable pulic support in my struggle.

I thought the choice of the title was good. Fetisov himself had suggested it, and the text supported it. But for Slava, it contained a land mine that exploded almost instantly.

Fetisov's stand was that the CSRA was the team of old and noble traditions, the team on which he grew up to be the best defence-man in the world. And now he wanted to move on, to try a new challenge, and should be allowed to do so. The hockey bureaucrats' position was solid and unbending: This was Tikhonov's team, which Tikhonov rules. You refuse to play for Tikhonov, therefore you are refusing to come forward for the CSRA. Good riddance to you.

But...

Suddenly, the very military officials who'd made him an officer in name only, as they'd named me, so we would be left totally free to toil for the CSRA and the National team, these people suddenly reminded him that he was a soldier. Since he was not playing hockey, Major Fetisov was now required to appear every morning at the club in his uniform, with his hair neatly cropped, and to hang around within its four walls. He had no duties, only lectures, threats, and word on the only possible way to conclude a truce:

"Viacheslav, make a public apology to Colonel Viktor Vasilevich Tikhonov and everything will normalize itself. You will be a hockey player again." Fetisov cut them short.

"Not for the world! I have nothing to apologize for. I wrote the truth."

Meetings began where the unyielding sportsman was "re-educated." The press was informed that the CSRA club unanimously had condemned Major V. A. Fetisov's behaviour.

Viacheslav clenched his teeth and refused to change his position. I don't accept everything he is, and don't agree with everything he does, which is natural. But this I know: He is a man of courageous character and a strong personality. He was not going to bend.

I had my own troubles. I'd been the first to openly engage in conflict with Tikhonov. Slava followed after me, but that did not make it any easier for him. Very likely, it made it even harder.

The heading on his article cut his chances in hockey and left him without realistic options to continue the fight. And the time was passing, and this super professional was losing his fitness edge for the game. I'd suffered from the lack of playing time just missing the IZVESTIA tournament in December, but at least I'd continued training. Through January and February, Slava was not allowed even to do that. It takes a long time to get into playing shape, especially when you are 30 years old. That conditioning vanishes very quickly with inactivity.

Still, Slava hung on.

In the newspaper SOVIET SPORT the interpretation of this conflict had, from the publication of my letter on, been strictly one-sided. There was a reason. His name was Leonid Trachtenberg.

Everything that had to do with hockey, and especially the select team, was covered for SOVIET SPORT by this famous reporter. And it is the right of a journalist to take up his own position, to be on one side or the other. But this experienced correspondent had a second assignment: He was also the official press attache of the U.S.S.R. National team, and therefore, was implicitly obedient to its senior coach, Tikhonov.

This is a man who can observe and report objectively, when he is in the employee of those on one side of the argument? It is the same as eating absolutely incompatible produce. You have to get sick. But not Trachtenberg. He did not even wince. He "mastered" both of his jobs. His aim was clear: To trave abroad with the National team, which would have a beneficial effect on his family's material budget. But surely one must also have a conscience?

Other press publications attempted to view the conflict objectively and argued for Fetisov, standing on the side of the hockey players for their elementary rights. Television also tried to be objective..

A curious thing happened during the a stop for an exhibition game in Sweden in 1989. After breakfast in the dining hall in the hotel, I opened a Stockholm newspaper and there, on the sports page, found a large photo of Fetisov and my brother Zhenya, wearing the uniform of the factory team "Sacco and Vancetti". I could almost see my brother doing that. First he fought for one team for the championship of the capital, now he played for another. Knowing his unstable character, this did not surprise me. But Fetisov, a world star, on a *factory team?*

There was a simple explanation: Fetisov was still fighting. He couldn't practice and train with CSRA while the issue was being resolved, so he accepted an offer from a coach he knew to train with the factory team when it rented the artificial ice of the Kristall training rink in Luzhniki. It made a sensational story and the Swedish correspondents in Moscow at the time for the world championships in "bandy" (an old and popular Soviet game, something akin to field hockey on ice, played outdoors), did not waste their opportunity to capture it.

Days passed, and weeks. Fetisov's name, one of the nation's favorite in sports in any case, was on the lips of millions, all of them awaiting in vain a quick resolution of the conflict.

During one of the rare evenings when I was at home, Fetisov's father telephoned me:

"Well, hello there, Igorek."

"Hello, Alexandr Maximovich."

"How are things going?"

"All right, I guess. Bearably. I will suffer until the end of the season, and then say farewell to all of this."

"So, why did you drop my Slava? How many years have you played together, played and seemingly were friends, and now the truth comes out? Slava is all by himself, taking the rap, and you keep on living the same way, and you do not give a care."

I was stunned.

"Maximovich, excuse me, I must interrupt. No one has dropped him. I personally will go with him to the end. Together. Do you believe me?"

"I would like to..."

"I give you my word. I swear with the health of my Alyonka, I will not leave Sasha!"

"May it be so, may it be so – but what is he supposed to do now? He is not playing, and he is no longer training. What will happen?"

"Do not worry, Maximovich. Just you wait. We will not give up that easily. We will think of something."

"Well, Igorek, keep your word. Good health to you."

"All the best, Maximovich. We will fight yet!"

Fetisov senior was terribly worried. In the beginning of the conversation he almost swore. By the end he was almost crying. I understood him very well. A couple of years ago, they had lost their youngest son, Tolya, in a car accident. He was a talented forward, already beating a path to the "base" of the CSRA. And here new troubles arose – the oldest son, their hope and support, in this terrible mess.

Typically, Tikhonov held two positions in the conflict with Fetisov. In an interview he declared: "No one threw Fetisov off the team." Behind the scenes he gave Viacheslav this ultimatum: "If you apologize publicly, I will forgive you everything. You will play again!"

Viacheslav refused. He could not do otherwise. After that, I understood that Fetisov would never appear in the uniform of the CSRA again.

The 1989 World Championship in Stockholm was drawing nearer. The voices in the press became louder and louder, calling for the return the captain of many years, into the ranks of the National team. Even the bureaucrats, it seemed, began to bustle about, earnestly interested in getting back the world crown that had been lost in Vienna. But here everything rested on the hockey monarch, namely Tikhonov. He avoided public appearances in every way possible. He still had not answered my letter from OGONYOK.

Instead of the hope shared by the fans and the members of the National team, the hope that somehow things would settle and that the opposing sides would at least make peace during the time of the World Championship, a feeling of despondency took over.

I could not accept that the train to Stockholm had already left without Fetisov. Especially because without our defenceman and leader, the hopes of a worthy performance on the ice of the specially built magnificent "Globen" arena would vanish. The National team is something special. In that I saw a way out, a way to return Viacheslav into our ranks.

Immediately after the last scheduled match of the championship of the Soviet Union, we, the National team members, were supposed to head straight to the Olympic training base at Novogorsk without going home. As soon as we had had our shower and changed, I approached Makarov and Krutov:

"Guys, we have to quickly drive to Ostankino. Let's the three of us give an interview on "Vzglad" (Point of View, the most popular television broadcast)."

"And what about the training camp? We will be late for the (11 p.m.) curfew," they both answered hesitantly.

"To hell with them, and with the training camp! This is a special situation."

"Yes, you are right. We could not care less about the curfew," said Krutov and Makarov, a little more confidently.

"Try to understand that this is the last opportunity to save Slava. To return him to hockey, to the National team. What a platform to tell everyone at least a little bit of what is really happening."

"Alright, why waste time talking?" Krutov said decisively. "Let's go!"

The interview aired two hours later, absolutely natural, without any cuts. Before millions of viewers, we briefly explained the situation, and in conclusion put forward the following harsh demand: either Fetisov be returned to the National team, or we, all of us, would not go to Stockholm, but would remain in Moscow, and that the second line of the National team – Khomutov, Bykov and Kamensky – was also supporting our ultimatum.

Another ultimatum! The third one this season. And what an ultimatum!

Tikhonov's response the next day in PRAVDA was a boast. If this is how things stood, then he would have to play without those two lines. There were plenty of good forwards in the country anyway.

It was a ridiculous stand, especially since he was constantly complaining about the lack of class players, and the narrow selection of candidates he always had for the National Team.

The National Team met in Novogorsk, and unanimously voted for the return of Fetisov. And Slava in his declaration to Kolosonov wrote: "My conflict with Tikhonov has nothing to do with the National team." In other words, he had said in the newspaper article that he would no longer play for Tikhonov *on the CSRA,* but would not let his feelings stand in the way of his duty and desire to perform for his country in the National team.

Tikhonov, the monarch, had to give in this time again.He tried hard not to admit to it. His right hand man, Trachtenberg, seached for phrases, for headings, for words in SOVIET SPORT which would create a totally different implication. But the counterbalance, a quite hefty one at that, was our ultimatum in the eyes of the enormous TV audience.

Again, he did not give in gracefully. He had another shot ready for Fetisov. No sooner had the National team arrived in Sweden than a new meeting was called – to elect a new captain!

There had been an incident in Kiev back in October, an encounter between Fetisov and the militia, for no apparent reason. Unfortunately, not one of the players was there with him, so I will not try to convince you of anything. I only know that our militia is far from irreproachable.

Slava later persistently fought for the dismissal of some sort of accusations that he broke laws. He even went so far as to have journalists conduct their own investigation. But while all of this was dragging on he received a formal military reprimand. Tikhonov immediately used his authority as a Colonel to appoint Makarov the new team captain, rejecting the players' requests for a free vote.

And now came the election of a captain for the World Championships.

It was not a difficult choice for National team players from other clubs. Makarov was the current captain. They were not involved with the years of shared searching for a candidate for the honourable duty of captain; the years of shared playing and finally friendship with Fetisov. For Krutov and me, it was a difficult and delicate situation. If we voted for Fetisov, we would involuntarily hurt Makarov, who did not deserve that. If we voted for Makarov, it would seem that the former years with Slava as captain meant nothing to us.

In the end that was the deciding factor. We had grown used to Slava being our leader, and we did not believe that he had somehow compromised himself as charged. We voted for Fetisov. And so he became the captain – by one vote!

And how he met the challenge and the responsibility!

He hadn't played for two months. But through colossal effort, digging to the very bottom of his enormous supply of talent, he gained conditioning with every match. When the tournament ended we had the championship back, and Slava was on the world all-star team and named as the tournament's best defenceman. With the money from this honor, he bought himself a bright red Volvo sports car. It must have driven Tikhonov crazy to see it.

Could anyone but Viacheslav Fetisov have done all this? I doubt it.

In a sense, he'd gotten the better of Tikhonov again. The senior coach's answer, as it was with me, was to cease to have any further contact with him. Another bonus!

It was the end of an unbelievable season, so full of conflict and turmoil one hardly had enough time to keep track of all the developments that were reshaping the lives of Soviet players and the game they loved.

The events in which Fetisov and I – and to a lesser degree Krutov and Makarov – participated, went out beyond the realms of purely internal conflicts in a team. This was not just between the players and the coach. The causes went a lot deeper, which is why the consequences were so far-reaching. But there was another consequence to come, and a fairly loud one at that.

We only had the early morning left in Stockholm. We rose at 6 a.m. and gathered at the bus, ready ahead of time as usual. Everyone had a lot more baggage than when we arrived. Besides the huge bags with the hockey gear, there were designer (label) clothes, electronic gear which the players bought with foreign currency received as bonuses for winning the championship. Five thousand dollars! For us, who were not spoiled by impressive honorariums, this was quite a lot of money.

We were collecting ourselves, getting into the bus, when our leaders noticed that something was missing. No, not a gold medal or a Japanese video cassette recorder. A man.

Mogilny was gone.

No one could explain what had happened. He'd been with the team the night before, behaved normally, and went into his room to rest.

To the moment of takeoff the delegation manager, Viacheslav Koloskov, was still hoping for something. And two days later the young CSRA and Soviet National team star was found, all right – in Buffalo, signing to play with the NHL Sabres, who had helped him to cross the ocean.

For our sports authorities, for our hockey fans and for the team it was a sensation. But given the player, it was hardly a surprise.

Mogilny is exceptionally talented, probably one of the more gifted of the new generation now appearing in Soviet arenas. He was also short-tempered, explosive, ambitious and sometimes unpredictable in his decision-making. He was also a reserved type who kept to himself. He came, trained with us, and he left. And what he lived by, except for hockey, no one even tried to find out.

Mogilny was born in the far east town of Khabarovsk, but clearly lacked any sort of provincial character traits. Quite the opposite. There was plenty of stubbornness in him, and insubordination towards authorities, including those of the CSRA.

He did not get along with Tikhonov at all. The coach dictator was driven to amazement and rage when confronted with all this jibbing and disobedience. Had he not been a winger of great range, he'd never have lasted. Veterans with titles under their belts usually behave themselves obediently. And here was this 20-year-old, battling him at every turn!

I remember such a characteristic episode. Mogilny had received some sort of small injury and the doctor freed him from the next match. But in the CSRA even the medical problems were finally decided by the senior coach. Sasha had planned to watch the game from the stands. But Tikhonov noticed him heading in the opposite direction from the locker room.

"Why are you promenading around?" he demanded. "Get changed on the double!"

Sasha countered in his imperturbable way:

"Doctor Silin freed me. I am not playing today."

"What? He freed you. But I am telling you, you are changing immediately and going on the ice! Otherwise you will be late for the warmup."

"I thought I had explained it clearly enough," Mogilny said, not giving an inch. "I will not play. That is all!"

And he headed for the stands. The distinguished hockey mentor had to bite his tongue, having even lost his gift of speech.

Their bickering had begun, I believe, back when Mogilny was enrolled in the main structure of the CSRA team, and according to the State registrar was listed as a private soldier. For them, the newcomers, their ration of the day consisted not of playing hockey, but just standing around calmly all day somewhere. We, the older players, sometimes helped them out: with money, or by inviting them out to a restaurant for the company so that they would not feel like strangers. We felt sorry for them. And Sasha, with his ambitions and his attitude, was already at that time not too impressed with the senior coach.

It probably came to a head at the Olympic Games in Calgary, where a shameful event occurred. Slava Fetisov witnessed it, and he would not lie.

During a tense moment in one of the matches, Tikhonov began to lay into Mogilny for his mistakes on the ice. As was his custom, he did not choose his words carefully. But, Mogilny was Mogilny. He did not agree with Tikhonov's reprimands and answered with a few words of his own. And Tikhonov hit him in the stomach!

So there was no mystery, really, as to why he had now fled. The escape of this talented player in many ways was predetermined by the circumstances that had been stewing in him day and night. The secluded country training camp got to him, as it had gotten to us veterans. Once his mother came to visit him, all the way across the country, but they would not let Sasha see her.

He didn't have his own apartment, either. They just kept feeding him with promises. Considering his relationship with the coach, he could hardly have believed in them. I myself remember Tikhonov's reply once when Sasha again snapped at some comment he'd made:

"I'll get you yet! As soon as this line leaves. I'll get to you. You'll dance yet!"

Knowing the vindictive nature of the hockey monarch, one could have no doubts that he would keep his word. Mogilny really had some "prospects" to look forward to. And there was something else. Sasha dreamed of some day playing in the NHL. But he saw how they harassed Fetisov, the famous Fetisov, for a whole year, while he had a ready contract. Such a prospect could hardly have enticed the young player him to stay.

I am not trying to justify him, but at the same time, I do not want to be a provocateur either. Each man's feelings for duty and country are his own and not to be forced on anyone. For all my battles I never thought to defect. How could I leave my mother and father? And friends? And Voskresensk? And the feeling of living in my own country?

It turned out that Alexandr Mogilny's escape was not such a sensation after all.

The first reaction of the CSRA bureaucrats was violent indignation: Mogilny was an army officer and thus a deserter. Therefore, he had committed a terrible crime! This I could not accept. He was hardly a military person! He was merely a boy forced to put on the uniform of the army if he wanted to play for the CSRA and the National team. A carbon copy of what happened to me in my own time. Nor did I believe that my few lines in my open letter in OGONYOK, where Mogilny was mentioned in haste, would get such a loud response.

But again, the most-used proverb of all: "There is no bad without good."

The escape of Mogilny was a great nuisance for our hockey. We had lost a player who at any moment was supposed to become a star. But this loss served to make the problem of mutual cooperation between our Hockey Federation and the NHL even more acute. Any further delays in the closing of the contracts between the Soviet and Canadian hockey clubs, and Mogilny might only be the first to go over the hockey wall. The fact that the Larionov Line is now scattered in the National Hockey League, to the profit of both themselves and the Soviet hockey system, shows at least that some sports managers had enough brains to draw a lesson from it.

Chapter 10
VICTORY

On May 23, 1989, seven months after the fateful article in OGO-NYOK and seemingly a lifetime since the 20-year-old boy had left his beloved small town to take that road to his hockey Rome, I became a civilian. On July 1, I signed a contract to join the Vancouver Canucks and test myself again, this time in the NHL.

For the Greens, for KLM, for the Larionov Line, there was another battle coming, but this time on a field of our choosing with rules that we knew and weapons we'd all spent our lifetimes mastering. How would we do in the NHL, with its smaller rinks and its incredible travel schedule and a game in which the aim was as often as much to ruin for rivals the swift flow of the sport we loved as to perform it yourselves? We didn't know – but we knew the whole hockey world, and particularly those in our homeland, would be watching.

Unfortunately, the four of us would not this time be fighting it together. Krutov would be with me, but the next time we met Makarov he would be a rival, a member of the Calgary Flames. And Slava? He would use his great talents for the New Jersey Devils. (In mid-season, in one of those curious turns of fate, he would also be united with Kasatonov, once his friend and defence partner, now a man with whom he shared nothing in common.)

But we were free of Tikhonov, free of the army. I had already been to Vancouver once, to familiarize myself with the city and the city with me. There were press conferences, meetings with players who would now be my teammates, a wonderful ocean fishing trip and even the taking of small sharks.

Until the contract actually was signed, it still seemed like one of those dreams that could be snatched away. I remember turning to the right in the region of the Sokol metro, on to the Leningrad Prospect and into the centre to the office of the firm Sovintersport

(Soviet International Sports). Involuntarily, I shuddered: Ah, was it possible? Would I wind up with CSRA again? But later, with the deal actually completed, I was as happy as a child: I could drive by the CSRA and not have to drop in!

But even before the possibilities of our being allowed to join the NHL were decided, there was one final task.

I do not consider myself to be a hockey revolutionary. It is just that I cannot be indifferent towards the work to which I have dedicated myself totally, and with which I am not planning to part in the future.

Sports is an area where everything is expressed clearly, distinctly. It shows the good that is in society, and also those points which torment it. And, as in politics and economics, there is a mass of problems stored up.

What has our pseudo amateurism alone cost us?

The bureaucrats and propagandists throw the dust into the people's eyes. They say that the Soviet stars are amateurs, that they are students, instructors of physical education and even laborers (!); and the stars of the West, our competitors, they are deep-rooted professionals.

Hockey is my professional work – but in Russia it is not a profession where innovation or change was encouraged or even allowed. One does not have to dig very deep in order to find an explanation for it.

For the bureaucrats, for the authorities, hockey has long-since become a beautiful banner behind which it was comfortable to sit quietly, doing nothing useful, but reporting at every opportune moment the great achievements of the Soviet hockey school in the international arena. But behind this banner a mass of problems has been growing steadily. With every year the interest of the fans falls catastrophically in our country. This does not worry anyone even today, except for us, the players, for who it is unpleasant to play in half empty arenas, and a few journalists not afraid to call things by their names.

Life is in full swing in soccer, in the last while. Many clubs have switched to self-sufficiency. The practice of drawing up contracts and the struggle for creating a professional soccer union has unfolded and has led – in July, 1989 – to the creation of the Professional Soccer League.

Through this, hockey remains in a state of a deep sleep. I cannot see any principle changes happening – no, not even in this time of peristroika and Gorbachev.

But that does not mean you must quit trying. When they informed me that the Hockey Federation of the USSR would be sitting the next day and wished me to speak, I cancelled my family outing to the cottage and began to get down on paper the thesis of my address.

At this meeting of those who controlled the fate of hockey in my country, I was the only hockey player present – and I'd come by choice. It would have been funny if it were not so sad. Such sad paradoxes were abundant in our hockey. In order to make clear the actual condition of our hockey and its inner organization, I will cite my speech in brief.

A good half of my five-minute monologue was dedicated to the deeds of Viktor Vasilevich Tikhonov. I then brought in a whole series of recommendations.

1. To create a hockey union, a professional unification of hockey players.

2. To implement a contract system for players and coaches, with clear directions as to the rights and responsibilities.

3. To create a hockey players' association, to attract all captains of the teams in the highest and first leagues.

4. To create a bill of rights for players' and coaches' travel abroad, with the money earned by the association through these tours and the transfer fees and share of our salaries to go only toward the development of hockey. (At that moment the question of Fetisov's, Makarov's, Krutov's and my going to the NHL was being decided. We had come up with the idea to direct a part of the received moneys towards the building of a factory, which would produce mainly equipment for children's hockey.)

5. To bring in the members of the USSR National team, Vyacheslav Bykov, and Vladimir Myshkin, into the ruling organs of the Federation.

6. To appoint Vladimir Alexeevich Yashenev as the executive director of the Hockey Players Association. He has been responsible for the education of the National team members for many years.

7. That the senior coach of the National team be without a team affiliation while coaching the National team.

8. That the Federation must be headed by a man who knows hockey and is devoted to it, preferably a former hockey player. I recommended Anatoly Vasilevich Firsov, a people's deputy and twice an Olympic champion.

Did anyone listen? In the near future the innovation of a players' contract is expected. A small beginning - but a beginning.